THE day I STOPPED BEING pretty

A MEMOIR

THE day I STOPPED BEING pretty

A MEMOIR

Rodney Lofton

SBI

STREBOR BOOKS

NEW YORK LONDON TORONTO SYDNEY

Strebor Books
P.O. Box 6505
Largo, MD 20792
http://www.streborbooks.com

ISBN-13 978-1-59309-123-1
ISBN-10   1-59309-123-0
LCCN 2007923865

First Strebor Books trade paperback edition October 2007

Cover design: www.mariondesigns.com

10 9 8 7 6 5 4 3 2 1

Manufactured in the United States of America

For information regarding special discounts for bulk purchases, please contact Simon & Schuster Special Sales at 1-800-456-6798 or business@simonandschuster.com

dedication

To my mother, thank you for loving me
when I didn't know how to love myself.

acknowledgments

To say that this journey has been an incredible one is truly an understatement of the term. As I reflect on where I have been, where I am and where the path is heading, I am truly thankful and blessed by the light that shines above me and within me. It has not been a piece of cake. As we grow, we live and we learn lessons that can either defeat us or make us stronger. For me, this journey has been both. But along with each bump in the road, there was a friend or a stranger to lend a hand of support, a shoulder to cry on or some type of nourishment to sustain this travel. It has not been a short trip and I hope that you will oblige me in thanking those individuals who have walked with me to keep me company, those who paved the way for my journey to be smoother and those who smiled to offer comfort along the way.

God, without you, I do not know where I would be. Through it all, You were there; every tear, every laughter, every bump and bruise. At times I lost my way, but You never allowed me to forget Your power, Your love and devotion. I thank You for the many gifts and blessings You have brought to my life. I thank You each day for Your love and the opportunity to see just one more day in Your beautiful creation. Thank You.

To my mother, the greatest gift I have ever known. When times were dark, you showed me the light. When love felt as if it had abandoned me, you were there to reassure me with your smile. When times were hard, with your love, you made it easier. I love you more than you will ever know.

To my Aunt Jettie, my kindred spirit. I will never forget the days of sitting in the Town, State and Colonial movie theaters with you and sharing the joy of movies and music with you. You planted a seed many years ago that continues to flourish in me. I love you. To my family, thank you for your love and support. Thank you for allowing me to dream and be me.

Family is not defined by the blood ties that we have. Family consists of individuals who come into your life and set up house. My extended family has been with me along this journey and it is only fair and fitting to thank them as well.

As a gay man, I think everyone should have a "Man DIVA" in their lives, and mine came in the form of Kevin Taylor. My friend, my brother, what can I say to you that I haven't said to you before? You have been a huge part of my life and I thank you so much. You have occupied and filled positions of friend, spiritual advisor, confidant, motivator and stern disciplinarian. You have laughed with me, cried with me and most importantly loved me. Your friendship is so pure. Thank you, DIVA. Thank you for encouraging me to "share my tr____" I love you.

To Karen Taylor-Bass, my sistah. Girl, you have been there with me through thick and thin. From the lean days of sharing black beans and yellow rice, to becoming the president of your own successful business venture, I celebrate the strong, black woman you are. Boyfriends come and go, but you will always be with me. I love you.

To my dawg, M'Bwende Anderson. I will never forget what you have done for me. You have been a friend during the highest of highs and the lowest of lows. Your friendship has been and continues to be a blessing to me. No one knows me like you do, both on the homefront and on the road. We will always have Tampa and New Orleans. Remember, I'm the one who tastes like Candy.

To Michael Green, twenty-two years and counting. From the early days of Scandals, to now, you have been there. When others turned away, or had something negative to say, you were there to celebrate me. You never criticized me, always encouraged me. You have been past, present and you will be part of my future. Thank you for your friendship.

To Shaun Ferrell. What started out as a casual hello has grown into a wonderful friendship. In a time when others have tried to cut me, you continue to have my back. Thank you for your friendship.

I have been blessed with "other mothers" over the years and it is important to acknowledge them and thank them for their love and nurturing. Ms. Blanche Williams, your home was always filled with love and you always extended that love to me. Thank you. To Ms. Marsha Logan, Morgan State seems so long ago, but you always went above and beyond your duties as my counselor; you became my friend. Ms. Diana Cooke, thank you for your love of not only me, but your friendship and love for my mother and family as well.

This life would be empty without the guidance of mentors. Dr. Ron Simmons, you are by far one of the most admirable and incredible men I have ever had the pleasure of meeting. I bask in your light. I drink in your knowledge. If I can become half the man that you are, my life here will not be in vain. Thank you for your guidance, your support and your sometimes brutal honesty. You are admired by many and loved by even more.

To Daphne Rankin, it is because of you my passion for HIV/AIDS work thrives. A chance meeting with you years ago showed me the joy in giving and sharing, thank you. To Mr. John King and Mrs. LaVerne King, thank you for healing my broken wings and showing me how to fly again.

I have been fortunate enough in this life to meet friends who may not be close in area, but definitely cemented their place in my heart. To Regina King, thank you for your continued support of my every endeavor. Your beauty shines through on screen and through the telephone when our schedules allow moments of sharing. No matter where you are or what you are doing, you always come through for a brotha and I love you. To Lynette Jones, some time has passed since our last conversation, but my love for you still continues. To Tyreese McAllister, when I grow up, can you teach me how to be like you? I love your spirit and take-no-prisoner attitude. To Cassandra "Baby Butch" McPherson, you are the bomb. I admire your commitment to young people and to self. Thank you all for gracing me with your love, your light and friendship.

There are so many others to thank. But before I go any further, I would like to thank the Strebor Books Family. To both Zane and Charmaine Parker, words cannot begin to express my deepest gratitude to the two of you for this opportunity, for taking a chance on me and allowing me to share with readers my journey. Thank you so much. To my sistah ghurl Ms. Tina Brooks McKinney, thank you for taking me under your wing and sharing with me what to expect on this new path. Marsha Jenkins-Sanders, you are beauty personified. Our paths have crossed for a reason. You are the spiritual reassurance when I sometimes get off path. Thank you, love. To Shelley Halima, Mija, I continue to enjoy our late-night conversations of life, love and everything under the sun. Thank you for just being you. To Lee Hayes, the voice that makes you melt. Your journey has paved the way for me and I thank you for taking me along for the ride. Laurinda Brown, why did you leave me here in Virginia? You are only a telephone call away, but it feels like you are right next door. Thank you for everything. To the rest of the Strebor Family, thank you for embracing me and offering insight and help. It is most appreciated.

I wouldn't be where I am if it weren't for those who came before me. To my grandmother, I miss you so much. Life has not been the same since you were called home. I miss playing Pitty Pat with you and having you happily take my money. I keep the ivory domino pieces and your wedding band to remind me of your beauty. When I see you next, I look forward to sitting down and pulling out those dominos. I love you, Grandma. To the numerous lovers, friends and loved ones who were called home much too soon; your place in my heart will never be filled. When you all left, you left a missing piece that has yet to be filled. I know that you all are watching me, smiling over me and making sure that your stories and lives will not be in vain. I miss you all.

To all the men I have loved. This was a difficult decision to share with others the love that we shared, but in order to heal and move on, this was my chance to do so. Thank you all for the love and the lessons you taught me. I treasure each and every one of you.

To the creative folks that made me look good when I didn't feel pretty,

Scott Stewart, for your great creative eye. To Anthony Cutajar for making me look handsome during the photo shoot and to Cheezi for hooking a brotha up with the right cut, thanks a million. To George, wherever you are, thanks so much for the myspace site.

I would also like to give a special thank-you to Juan Pierce and the staff of the Minority Health Consortium, for your support. A special hello to the folks at the United States Postal Service, Floyd Avenue Station: Singh, Janice, Jackie, Mr. George, Mr. Booker, Abel, Big Lou and the rest of the carriers, who taught me how to "not run a route."

To the friendly faces and the backstabbers at Bar Code. You all know which categories you fall in. To my hanging partners, Rufus Edmonds, Ronald Drake and Kevin Pollard, you guys make life in Richmond a lot more tolerable.

A special shout-out to Terrence Jones, I still hold a place for you in my heart. For twenty years we shared a great deal; maybe when time heals the wounds that have driven us apart, we will be able to share once again.

There are so many others to thank, but not enough space here. Please know that you are not excluded from my thoughts. Your contributions to my life have left an indelible mark and I thank you.

And last, but certainly not least, to my late father. I know now that you loved me, the only way you knew how. I can't take back what was said, nor can I dwell on what wasn't said. Please know that I thank you for the man that you were. It is because of you that I am here and that is something to love and embrace. If I have one regret, it is that I didn't tell you I loved you when you were with me. I tell you now, I love you, Dad.

introduction

How did I get here? My head was pounding from the bright overhead lights. My throat was sore from the induced vomiting brought on by the nasty liquid charcoal I was forced to drink. The strangers I encountered reminded me of the days I lived in New York, cold and distant, rushing about to take my pulse and temperature. I wanted to yell and tell them to leave me the fuck alone, but all I could muster was another dry heave. How did I get here? I thought. The last few hours had become a blur. I remember hearing the words of Chante Moore dancing in my thoughts by the candles lighting the living room of my apartment. The shadows from the candles appeared strangely erotic on the walls of the basement apartment as I listened over and over to the lyrics, *"The world going by my window, doesn't mean nothing to me. Why do I feel the way I do, why am I still so lost in you."* As I sat there with my favorite bottle of liquid courage, I reached for the bottle of pills I had stored up for this moment. I remembered the doctor saying they would relax me and allow me to sleep. I never had taken them before. I just waited until the end of each month to have the refills ready for this moment. Hell, if truth be told, I really didn't want to bother with taking any more pills on top of the numerous multi-colored pills I took daily just to live in this hell of an existence. As I built up the nerve to take the next step in an already tragic life, I realized that the ice had melted and watered down the rum in my glass. I didn't care. It would decrease the chances of the ice entering my mouth along with the pills. So, I reached for the almost empty fifth of Bacardi and filled my glass. Chante's voice continued to sing to my broken heart, *"as if we never met."*

I thought it would be difficult to swallow all of the pills at once, but the lifestyle I had led had taught me well. The first handful disappeared without as much as a gag. Then the second handful followed. I washed them down with the room-temperature rum and sat back for the ride. As my thoughts became cloudy and incoherent, I reached for the telephone. I wanted to wait just long enough before I called anyone, knowing that the pills had taken their toll on my body, waiting eagerly so that the survival rate would be slim to none. I wanted a couple of important people to know that I was no longer going to have trouble sleeping. I was going to finally have that one true great sleep that had deprived me all these years.

The next thing I remembered was the blaring of the ambulance siren ducking and dodging traffic to get me to the emergency room. Once again, my sleep would be interrupted. I lay there in the hospital's emergency room, dry spittle forming at the corners of my mouth, clothes disheveled and praying that I had followed my mother's advice of wearing clean underwear. And all I could think about was, *how did I get here?*

To say that I am the average thirty-something would be lying. I've lived many lifetimes in the life Father/Mother/God has blessed me with. From traveling the world to rubbing elbows and exchanging bullshit with the rich and famous. From being kept by a rich and powerful man, even if it was in his own mind, to sleeping in a sleazy pay-by-the-hour motel in New York City's Greenwich Village. From the state senator to the grocery store manager, I've entertained them all and then some. To each of them, I was the pretty young face that held on to their every word. I listened attentively as they told stories of their lives and loves. I yearned to visit the places they described and sample the foods and drinks they experienced. I was the young impressionable "mama's boy" paying careful attention to their every movement, every gesture, so at some point down the road I could imitate them. I would model my walk, my talk, my style of dress after each one; they were good teachers and I had always been a good student.

I was also the tight ass they sought pleasure and comfort in. If by chance that didn't do it for them, my mouth was willing to complete the task and carry the load, no pun intended. Either way, they relieved themselves of all of their daily frustrations. In doing so, what was something that was once sacred and forbidden, became a pounding spot for their manhood. Big, small, thick or thin. My needs were secondary to theirs. Once their energy was depleted, they would quickly yawn, turn over and go to sleep. I wanted so desperately to be held after I gave so much of myself to them. I would reach out to them, only to be told, "I have to get up early."

In the beginning, I found myself swallowing the sobs and pre-cum as I turned over to gather my thoughts. I would sometimes lie awake thinking to myself, *Why didn't he respond? I just did what he asked of me. Why can't he just hold me in his arms?*

I found this scenario playing out over and over again throughout my life. Always giving of myself, my emotions and my body until there was nothing left. After the draining of me, it inevitably led up to the end. I was always on the receiving end: "This isn't working for me," or "I'm feeling suffocated." And there I stood each and every time with tears streaming down my face, broken-hearted, a bruised and sometimes battered asshole, asking the question, "Why?" What did I do wrong? I told him, whoever he was at the time, I loved him. I showed him, not just with my body, but with my words. He felt it from my heart, he saw it in my eyes, and it was clearly demonstrated in my actions. I replayed the scenes over and over. There I stood center stage in my monologue, spotlight on me and confessing "I want to be with you" and hearing in exchange, "Sorry." As the curtain closed and the emotion-filled show was over, I stood there alone.

And as I stand here alone pondering what you may think, I'm feeling open and honest to tell you my role in those relationships that have shaped me today. Some of you may find my existence a sad one, and at times, it was and has been. I'm feeling that some of you may find it too brutally honest and the remainder will just shake their heads and *tsk, tsk* me. It's the story of my life: the good, the bad, and the oh so very ugly. The lives I have led and the lives I have destroyed because I thought I knew love. You'll heave of the loves I truly loved and lost. You will hear the stories of those who were only there for the moment. But it is all, my truth.

You will hear the memories of growing up, the ugly emotional and physical scars and the hopes that things will be better tomorrow. Some, if not all of you, will find this story graphic, but there is no other way to tell it. It has to be told the way it was lived, every sordid and painful detail. So I will apologize to those of you now for offending you. Please believe me, it was never my intent. It is my goal to open my heart and soul to you not for your compassion or understanding, but more so for my own personal healing. I am not soliciting, nor do I want your pity, because everything that has happened to me has been of my own doing. I take responsibility for my actions. I am not here to lay blame on anyone. But be advised, there were supporting players and contributors to my life of love, happiness, anguish, and pain. You will not hear about all of them, there were far too many to count. But you will hear about the key figures that played a pivotal role in my great rise and fall and my future ascension.

I want you to sit back and relax. Adjust the lights to your mood and enjoy your favorite drink of choice. Take in what I say and how I say it. It all comes from the heart. There is no laugh track that goes along with this story, so if you feel like laughing at something, please do. On the other hand, if you feel like crying, I invite you to do so. In the time that I have been here, I have done both, so it's okay.

Thank you for taking time to listen. You are about to embark on my journey on how I got to this place. So enjoy, learn something, laugh, cry, but most importantly, live.

chapter one

I remember the first time I fell in love, or discovered the hurt associated with the word *love*. In my eyes, at that time, he was the greatest man I had known. Handsome as all get out. He was a beautiful high-yellow man with a voice that commanded my attention each time he opened his mouth. His hair was jet-black and wavy, with a hint of premature gray at the temples. If models ever sought their inspiration for poses and clothing styles, they looked no further when they saw him. He was my guy. The only fault he possessed was his emotional distance. He would only allow me the pleasure of his time when he wanted to. His telephone calls were few and far between. If and when he had time for me, I dropped everything and everybody to be with him.

Upon receiving the call that he was ready to grace me with his presence, I found myself running around frantically to search for the right outfit. He made sure that I was presentable to be with him by purchasing the right looks that he thought suited me. Jeans were never allowed when we spent our time together. So I searched the closet high and low for an outfit that he especially liked seeing me in. I dusted off the Stacy Adams he had purchased for me to wear with the special evening attire.

I would shower until my skin had pruned. I wanted to make sure that there were no visible signs of dirt or grime. After toweling dry, I prepared myself the way he showed me. I moisturized my skin, so that if I was lucky enough to receive a hug from him, he would feel the softness of and know immediately I was taking care of myself. I would apply a light dab of hair cream to my own curly locks. I didn't want him to feel the grease of the Ultra Sheen I usually used. He would not like that. After brushing my teeth and applying a liberal, yet small amount of his favorite cologne, I made my way to the living room to await his arrival. *He'll be here shortly*, I thought. I didn't want anything to mess up the evening we were about to share.

As I looked up at the clock, time had passed and he was more than forty-five minutes late. Each time I heard a car horn blow or a door slam shut, I rushed to the window to see if it was him. No sign of him yet. It shouldn't have surprised me, I was used to this. If this was the only way to be with him, it had to be. Almost one hour and fifteen minutes to the time he stated that he would be here, he finally showed up. He lacked the Southern charm and mannerisms of men I would encounter after him. He just laid on his car horn to signal me to come out. I checked myself once again in the mirror to make sure that everything was just right for him.

As I made my way to the top-of-the-line Cadillac he had recently purchased, I rehearsed my script for this moment. I would not comment about his tardiness. I would simply smile that smile that disguised my hurt and act as if he had actually showed up on time. This gift of disguising my hurt and pain would figure prominently in my later years. I would eventually become a master of appeasing others, yet continuing to lie to myself. I reached for the handle of the car door and took my place on his silent command next to him. Although I was disappointed and knew that our evening would be cut short due to his late arrival, I mustered up a smile and simply said, "Hi, Dad."

My earliest memories of my father are vague and a little blurred. From the beginning of our relationship, I remember my mother sending me off with this man that she explained was my other parent. My mother bundled me up tightly, the oversized scarf covering my small face and the mittens placed on my petite hands. She sat me down and explained to me that I would be spending the weekend with this man and to be on my best behavior. I nodded my head in anticipation as she handed me my travel bag and answered the door.

He stood there as I looked up at him. He was a giant in my eyes and a foreigner to me. He ran his fingers through my hair, as he explained to me along with my mother that I would be spending the weekend with him and his new family. It was the end of the Christmas holiday season. He and my mother exchanged pleasantries as he shuffled me out of the door toward his waiting car. I wanted to cry because I was leaving the only parent I had known up until this point, but sensing my fear, my mother placed a kiss on my cheek and told me it would be okay. She always had a way of knowing how I felt without me telling her. She stood in the doorway of our two-bedroom corner apartment until I made my way to the car and my father made his way out of the parking lot. I watched as my mother became a small dot as this man and I made our way down the hill heading toward his home, his family, his world. Riding through the neighborhood, I noticed my friends playing with their new toys, riding new bicycles minus the training wheels we had outgrown, and playing with baseball gloves we had all asked Santa to bring us. I wanted to jump out of the car and make my way over to them, but I was secured by the seatbelt and the curiosity of knowing this man that barely spoke a word.

The ride was a fairly quiet one, with an occasional question here and there. The majority of the dialogue came from the radio that played the same Christmas carols I had grown tired of some weeks earlier. I would periodically look out the window as I noticed the scenery change at every turn. In my neighborhood filled with single mothers attempting to make little boys into men, struggling to make ends meet, there weren't playgrounds for the kids. But as we continued this silent journey, I noticed the large playgrounds that provided swings and merry-go-rounds. I noticed the concrete pavements we played Rollie Pollie on, were now replaced by perfectly manicured lawns. Even with the chill in the air, the grass seemed rich in color and withstood the blustery cold we had to endure that year.

We continued our road trip and I found myself stealing glimpses of this man. So this was my father, I thought. He doesn't look like me. But he is the same color as I am, maybe just a shade lighter. I wouldn't mind looking like him when I got older, I told myself. I redirected my attention to the road. The apartment that I called home was now replaced with nice little cardboard houses with front yards and neatly decorated lawns of reindeer and snowmen. The trash that littered the streets and cracked sidewalks where I lived were now replaced with smooth paved walkways and clean streets. After about twenty-five minutes, we arrived at his house.

He grabbed my small overnight bag as we made our way to the front door. "Della, I'm back," he called out as he entered. I looked around at the gifts around the garishly decorated Christmas tree and the expensive furniture. I was hoping as every kid does around the holiday season that some of the gifts under the tree were for me. I squinted to make out some of the names on the big colorful presents, hoping to see one or two presents from Santa for me. My inspection of the packages were interrupted when she walked in.

To best describe her physical appearance, imagine a female version of Verdine White of Earth, Wind and Fire. She was a little darker than my father and obviously older. She wore an apron around her waist and from the smell in the air, I knew she had made her way out of the kitchen. Even at this early age, I could tell that she did not want me there. She coldly greeted me. As my eyes darted back to the gifts, her voice snapped me back to this reality as she took my coat. Following my mother's instructions of being polite, I said "thank you." As she disappeared into yet another room to hang up my coat, I continued to survey my new surroundings. All around me were pictures of teenagers and kids that appeared to be around my age. I would find out later that the framed photographs were pictures of her, my father, her children and grandchildren. As she explained to me who each one was and what they did, I noticed something was missing: a picture of me.

I was guided to a back room that contained more Christmas presents but not as many as in the living room. These were gifts that were selected, purchased and delivered by Santa just for me. The wrapping wasn't as nice, nor were the packages as big as the ones underneath the tree in the living room, but I said "thank you." I always played by the rules. I started to unwrap the gifts and attempted to disguise my hurt in what I received from Santa Claus and this man. There were clothes, underwear, socks and the necessities that every child needed during the winter season. The only toy in any of the boxes was the board game Trouble. Before dinner and bedtime, we played a few games and exchanged light banter about school. I was encouraged to take a bath and prepare for bed after dinner. Heavens forbid I dirty her sheets.

As I lay there listening for something in the quiet night air to remind me of home, I thought about my mother and cried. I wanted to be with her. I remembered her smile as she waved to me and I wrapped that smile around me that night and held on to it. This was only the beginning of infrequent trips and future heartbreak from this man who walked into my life. But as I did that night, in wrapping myself in my mother's smile, that smile would be used to get me through some of the darkest days I would face in the future.

This man I started to call Dad had an off-hand approach to raising me. His idea of fatherhood consisted of a monthly child support check in the amount of $40. Sometimes it came on time, sometimes it was late. My father was also void of any emotions. Not until I was sixteen years old, did I ever see him cry. For some reason, I always thought there was a manual boys received at an early age to teach them how to be men. Those lessons that shaped me and molded me were handed down to me from the women in my life, not from my father. The simple lessons, mind you, like holding the door for a lady, or saying "thank you." I was taught to say, "May I?" versus "Can I?" by the women in my life. I never received the complete male version of life's rules from good old Dad. However, my father decided there were certain things a man needed to know that were not included in his own pocket version. Those lessons, in his cold way, prepared me for the others I would encounter.

chapter two

While growing up, I was always called "pretty." At an impressionable age, I assumed that being pretty was a good thing. Hell, I was taught being high yellow or redbone were both terms of endearment. Combined with light skin, my head was covered with what my mother affectionately called "shit-colored brown locks." To my mother, cutting my hair was shameful. As I look back on the many class pictures of yesteryear, I finally realize what she meant. I had a head full of hair that even some of the neighborhood girls envied. I was taught by my father to be the little heartbreaker, but no one shared with me how powerful the word *pretty*, when used the wrong way, could hurt so much.

During the rare moments I spent with my father, I became a showpiece for him, as opposed to his true desire to want to be with me. Although he was married to Della and not my mother, my father was known, as we say in the South, as a cock hound. At an early age, I found myself being pimped by my father in order for him to meet other women. Like a vulture circling his prey, my father would allow me to roam a safe distance from him. I was always within his view. If we were attending a family gathering or invited to a barbecue, I found myself running and laughing with the newfound cousins I had just discovered. I had to be careful not to get dirty while out with my father. Playing in dress slacks and lace-up shoes didn't go over too well with the other kids. Even though I couldn't really enjoy playing with the other cousins the way I wanted to, I was with my father and that was the most important thing to me, for these moments didn't happen very often.

As I made my way around the fenced-in backyards or seeking out something to drink or eat, women would approach me. I had the hair, I had the skin complexion, and I had my father's genes. I engaged these women with my smile and my perfect manners. And without fail and with his keen sense of smell for the kill, he would swoop in at the right time. I was the bait that he used to snag the catch. Once my father introduced himself to these unsuspecting women, I was prompted to move on and go play, but with the knowledge not to get dirty. This was not the quality time I had in mind when he said he wanted to see me. He was the only one who benefited from these little get-togethers.

I eventually got older and the relationship between my father and me continued to change. I assumed with this newfound maturity that we would develop a stronger bond. I chalked up his ability to detach himself emotionally from me was due in part to his fear that I would abandon him in some way. Boy, was I reaching for a reason to justify his behavior. At every turn I found myself making excuses for him and forgiving him, but he remained the same. I learned quickly that my father wasn't incapable of loving; he just decided when and with whom he wanted to share that love with.

The very few moments my father dedicated to me were stretched even more when my mother decided to pack me up and move to Baltimore. My father didn't put up a struggle to gain custody or even fight it. He gave my mother his enthusiastic support and assured her the monthly child support checks would continue. Although he had no real role in my day-to-day rearing, he was no longer obligated to set aside any real time for me. He was given a golden opportunity to avoid playing any significant role in my life from this moment on. As with his other kids he had by three other women, he left me alone and abandoned. He was free to be. But before he allowed me to go, he needed me one last time, once more for old time's sake. But of course, it wasn't to be with me. This last time together would change my life and the way I viewed myself from that moment on. It also changed how I allowed others to view me as well.

It was my aunt and uncle's twenty-fifth anniversary. It was a time of celebration, but in hindsight, it was an opportunity for her to showboat for her friends and less fortunate relatives. This was the first time I ever saw her splurge on anything. She spared no cost at impressing her invited guests. She was the type of woman who pinched a penny until Lincoln screamed. I never received anything new from her during our visits to her home. I was the recipient of bags of clothes previously worn by my cousin. There was no mistaking they were his hand-me-downs, his name was written with a bold black magic marker so that I would never forget where they came from. That included his used and sometimes tattered underwear. She had a way of making me feel inferior to her son because he came from a two-parent stable home. When visiting her, I would have to endure discussions of how wonderful he was doing in sports. He was very athletic. Because she worked in the school system, it didn't help my cousin much since he was diagnosed with dyslexia; however, I was Johnny on the spot, and always asked to spell a word. When I spelled it correctly, my accomplishments were placed aside to focus the attention once again on her son. I couldn't win a place in my father's heart and with her being his sister, I knew I would never have a place there either.

My father and I traveled to my aunt's river place for the big celebration. Many of the people in attendance were unfamiliar faces to me. I did, however, spot my other aunt who had a penchant for white men. This sister of my father donned blonde wigs to hide the hair that was a product of her darker-hued father, my grandfather. The wigs blended beautifully with her pale skin, giving the illusion that she was truly a white woman of leisure. It was rare that I saw her, but I was happy to see her. She treated me better than my dad's other sister. Aunt Lacey introduced me to the new man in her life, Larry. She showered me with accolades, as she commented on how clean I looked, how well dressed I was, and how beautiful my hair was groomed. Remembering what my mother had told me about being polite, I said, "thank you."

Like a trained seal, I maneuvered through the crowd, playing up to all for their amusement and delight. As I had many times on the rare occasions with my father, I took center stage to impress him. But this time, rather than be silently thanked for landing another potential fuck for him, I felt his wrath.

There she was—a different face, a different dress, a different smile, but the catch was the same. She would be the next in a line of women to smile and pinch my cheek. Her hand would be soft once again as she stroked my face to compliment me, "You are so pretty." I looked around, knowing that my father was not too far away and ready to swoop down. "Thank you," fell from my small mouth on cue.

And there he was. I prepared myself to exit this scene as I had many times before, to allow my father his fifteen minutes to shine, to run his game. But this time was different. Rather than motion me off, my father showed the most emotion I ever had seen him display. He grabbed me about the arms and abruptly shook me. I was stunned by his display in front of this woman, but sadistically happy at his release of his emotions. He then provided me with some insight of his rage. "Men are not pretty, men are handsome and don't you forget it!" My head was swirling. *Had I done something wrong? But this is what you taught me, what you always told me. I was the pretty little boy you created.* I tried to read and comprehend his anger, but it never happened. I had grown accustomed to my father's lack of feelings, but this outburst in front of this woman and strangers alike made me want to cry. With a tremble in my voice, I managed to say, "Yes, Sir."

From that moment on, I measured my self-worth based on what my father said to me that day. I began a journey searching for my father's missing and elusive love, whenever and wherever I could find it. That was the day I stopped being pretty.

chapter three

It was a Saturday when the move came. My mother had been in Baltimore for a month to set up house. On a trip to visit family, she had fallen in love with Waddell, an older gentleman she had met at the Elks lounge. They maintained a long distance romance for some time, before he asked her to move to Maryland.

Outside of my own father, I never had a male role model, or figurehead, in my family. The men in my family were either incarcerated, or neglected the kids they spawned. So it took some time for me to adjust to having another "man," outside of me, in the household. Waddell had come to visit several times and took these moments to impress me. Although I was young, I could tell my mother was happy. She had placed her own happiness on the back burner for me and it was now time for her to experience the love she deserved. God knows she didn't receive it from my father. She was twenty-three when she gave birth to me and assumed that she would marry my father. Unfortunately, after my birth, she received a call from my father's sister one night, informing her of the news.

During the time that my father was courting my mother, he was seeing someone else, Della. My paternal grandparents assumed that my father would make my mother part of their family, but that never happened. My aunt made the tearful call. Lil' Joey had gotten married. Any hopes of a lifetime together for my mother and father were dashed and she focused her love and attention on me. Now Waddell was the new man in her life.

She was happy and I was happy for her.

Waddell's silver Cadillac came to a halt in front of the place we would call home. It was definitely an adjustment for me. I was used to sharing a room with my little cousin Andy, his feet resting in my face as we slept on opposite ends of the twin-sized bed. Now, I was alone in my own room. I had my own television that I didn't have to fight to view, and a bed that I could truly enjoy without waking up in Andy's piss.

I missed my family back in Richmond, but I was home now in Baltimore. I started to make friends and I really enjoyed school. I was finishing my last year of elementary school and heading toward junior high. I started to grow more, noticing the changes in my body, the spurts of hair growing on my body and understanding what having a father figure was like in my life. Although Waddell was sometimes a strict disciplinarian, he was there. He replaced the emptiness I felt when I saw my other friends with their fathers. I found myself laughing at his corny jokes and silently celebrated the love he placed in my mother's heart. I felt good, this felt good. But in the back of my mind, my dad still lurked.

Yes, he was still present. The checks came as he'd promised. On visits to Richmond during summer vacation before the start of the new school year, I was sometimes fortunate enough to see him for a few hours when he and Della took me school shopping. But outside of those moments, our contact was very limited, or initiated by me, with a card mailed to him on Father's Day or his birthday. Not until I turned thirty-three, did he ever call me on my exact birthday. It was usually two or three days later. Although I never shared with anyone how I felt, I became the great pretender. I never allowed anyone to see the hurt I felt in not having him in my life the way I wanted. Now that I was on the brink of becoming a teenager, I realized that the relationship or lack of relationship we shared would be reminiscent of the one we shared when I was a child—non-existent.

ʂɔⳆʂ

I was excited at the prospects of entering high school. I always assumed that once you entered high school, you were a few short steps away from being an adult. Life in Baltimore was good. I had been living there for five years now and was ready for my first day of my sophomore year. From the ground running, I needed to establish myself in high school. I didn't want to get lost among the other incoming sophomores. Being and living in Baltimore was very different from anything I had remembered growing up in Richmond. The last class I attended in Richmond only possessed two white students, one girl and one boy. My first day of high school in Baltimore, I was now part of the minority, where I was once part of the majority.

High school was supposed to be fun. I was to learn about life and make wonderful lifetime friends. Unfortunately, I only encountered the bigoted stares and taunts of the white students I shared classes with during the day on my walks home from school. During the seven or eight hours we spent together five days a week, we were cool, the best of friends. Soon as the school bell rang to end the day, I became an invader in their community. I didn't receive much support from my black friends. To them, my participation in extracurricular activities like Student Council or Drama Club, constituted my desire to be white.

But they didn't understand. I had a hidden agenda. Although I didn't talk to my father much, I wanted to share with him, on those rare moments, my accomplishments in high school. I wanted him to be proud of me. I wanted to hear in his voice over the 150 miles that separated us, that he was proud. It didn't happen. No matter what I accomplished, like becoming president of my sophomore class, my father wasn't easily impressed or very much interested. I clearly had not displayed any athletic prowess while growing up and my dad was only interested in sports achievement. During our brief conversations, I couldn't talk to him about what the Orioles or the Colts were doing, nor could we talk about the arts, which became a passion of mine. I attempted to pick happy mediums that we could address, but to no avail. No matter what I shared, he was not receptive. It appeared the only thing that added any perk to my father's voice were questions or topics regarding girls.

My experience with girls was very limited. At the age of fifteen, I had very little interest or attraction toward girls. I didn't think there was anything wrong with that. I was focused on school and trying to make something of myself. Now, don't get me wrong, there were girls I liked being around and girls I thought were cute, but that was it. I was too busy joining the numerous after-school programs. Every now and then, I would meet a girl with whom I shared some commonalities and would even engage in the art of pressing clothes, or bumping and grinding, but I didn't really know what I was doing. My few neighborhood friends tried their best to get me to do so much more with the girls I met, by professing to me the joys of penetration. I wasn't interested until she walked back into the picture.

chapter four

E very summer since I moved from Richmond to Baltimore, I looked forward going back to Richmond to see my family, especially my grandmother. Grandma was like everything you could want in a home. She was laughter and love. She was that extra cup of sweetness that made you want so much more. I looked forward to waking up every morning and sitting at the kitchen table, where the night before she served up half-pints and pints of Early Times to the local neighborhood customers. With a half-gallon of Early Times, she tripled her return by jacking up the price for convenience.

Her business savvy didn't stop there. Without fail, some customers would goad Grandma into a card game, whether it was Tonk or Pitty Pat. She would reach down in her bank, also known as her bra, and retrieve the crinkled dollar bills her customers had just given her to clear their books from a weeklong of complimentary drinks. Food was in abundance, as she knew alcohol mixed well with fried fish and chicken dinners. The kitchen table was now reminiscent of the Las Vegas casinos, with a little bit of grease having to be wiped away from the cards.

Yes, I couldn't wait to sit there each morning for the next few weeks and watch meticulously how my grandmother moved about. My cousins and I would sit there eagerly waiting for breakfast. The lopsided pancakes were smothered with Karo syrup heated in a pan of water. There were no microwaves at the time. Fried bologna with just the right amount of burn and the scrambled eggs fried in the same skillet as the bologna. Grandma always had Maxwell House Instant Coffee and a Salem cigarette for breakfast. If we were good and ate the delicacies placed in front of us, she would pour a little coffee in the saucer for us to sip. My cousins preferred the taste of milk. Personally, I liked the little sip of coffee from Grandma's cup. I felt like I was drinking from the cup of a goddess. The nights were even better. Huddled around the foot of Grandma's easy chair, we stole glances of her peeling apples with the dull steak knife. Between fighting for control of what to watch on television, my cousins and I would beg Grandma for a slice of apple. It was easy for us to have her peel one for us, but we each fought for the first piece. Grandma used to tease us about being greedy when she performed this ritual each night before bedtime. "Just like a dick in a whore house," she would say as she smiled and doled out slivers of her apple. Oh, how I would give anything to see that smile and hear her voice again. I truly miss her.

൮൙

It was the summer before I entered my junior year in high school and I prepared for my annual visit to Grandma's. After three unsuccessful attempts, I had finally passed the written portion of the driver's exam and had planned to work with my great-uncle that summer to purchase a car. I would be turning sixteen a week after returning to school for my junior year and I wanted a car. I was tired of being called "nigger" on the walks home from school and this was my way of getting what I wanted.

I knew working for and with my great-uncle would be the equivalent of slave labor. He believed strong in a hard day's work with minimal pay. He did reassure me that whatever I saved and if I showed initiative, he would help me. I wasn't used to working for anything that I wanted. If there was something I wanted or desired, all I had to do was ask my mother for it. Money was not flowing in my household, nor were we poor, but if there was something I pleaded for, my mother would sacrifice her own wants and needs for my own selfish wants. This time I wanted to do it on my own. I would spill blood, sweat and tears this summer to achieve my goals. I had entertained the thought of asking my father. It was a hope that we could go car shopping together once I had the money and share that time together, but now being closer to him in Richmond over the summer vacation, he still didn't have time for me. Even now, our telephone conversations were short and neither of us had to pay long distance for the call. Unlike the days of waiting for his arrival when he called to say he was on his way, now that I was older, he no longer showed up late; he never showed up at all.

It's amazing how the mind can easily be distracted from the most important goals and tasks we set for ourselves. Every mapped-out plan I made after receiving my learner's permit on the third try flew quickly out the window when I saw my grandma's neighbor.

I remembered her immediately when I saw her. She still looked the same. Since our last encounter, I could tell that she had a hard way to go. She had been running from her own personal demons and she finally found her way back to an apartment located directly behind my grandma's house.

I wasn't good at reading anyone's face, but I knew through her fragile smile life had not been kind to her. Maybe it had been her romantic connection with my older cousin, who convinced her through his persuasive voice to show how much she cared for him by doing what he said, when he said it and how. I could only imagine the things he coerced her into doing. He taught me at an early age that, "Men were pimps and they take their money from their bitches." I guess that summed up his thoughts of her.

I found myself avoiding work with my great-uncle to spend time with her. As we sat and talked of life and where we had been and where we had hoped to go in life, I realized there was nothing I could do or say to heal her as a fifteen-year-old self-proclaimed man, barely out of puberty. What I did offer her was a kind ear. I knew what it was like to hurt for something that eluded you and wanting something you know you could never have. During these conversations, we shared our pain through forced laughter and silent moments. We spent hours on end together, to the point my great-uncle gave up on me and I gave up on getting the car.

During those conversations, she allowed me some time to share my life with her. I was guarded in what I revealed, making sure not to allow her too much insight into my feelings of abandonment and distance with my father. At times I found myself about to reveal a little too much of myself and reined myself in so not to appear too vulnerable.

One night during these moments of sharing, I allowed my heart to expose a little more than usual. She and I sat in her dark, heat-blistering apartment. The four walls seemed to be closing in on the two of us as we sat there. The only light illuminating the room came from the street-corner lights posted outside her front door. Her electricity had been disconnected and no relief was in her immediate future. We sat there in the stifling heat searching for comfort for our battered hearts and souls.

I was not an experienced lover. Up until that moment, my sexual experiences had been limited to two girls. The first was a bucktooth girl who told everyone in the neighborhood that sex with me ended before it began and that if felt like she was rubbing pussies with another girl. In defense of myself, it was my very first time. The second was a girl I met after helping an elderly lady with her groceries during a snowstorm in Baltimore. As my mother made her way to work the next morning, I was tasting the dirt on her unwashed titties. I was able to insert my fingers in her to see if what my neighborhood friends said was true, and sad to say, it was pretty bad.

After those two experiences, I mastered the art of masturbating. Initially, I didn't know what masturbation was until I had a physical to enter high school. My pediatrician at the time asked me if I played with myself, if I masturbated. I felt a tinge of disgust. I couldn't imagine at that time doing something like that. My doctor informed me that if I played with it, "it" being my dick, that I would go blind and grow hair in my palms. I vowed never to do it. As we do with our buddies, I shared this conversation with my friends. My buddies laughed and told me otherwise.

Armed with an old *Hustler* magazine and instructions, I went home and locked my bedroom door. I proceeded to turn the television on so that if there were any noises coming from me, the pre-programmed laugh tracks of my favorite television shows would muffle them. Following the instructions, I grabbed the ninety-nine-cent bottle of Aquamarine lotion I loved.

I flipped the pages of the magazine until I came across a picture that caught my attention. It was loosely based on the Sam Cooke song, "Frankie and Johnny." I wasn't so much impressed by the layouts of the centerfold, but I was intrigued at the sight of this man and woman frolicking. I rose to the occasion. As I took myself in my hand, I applied the lotion. It was a bit cool from the cool room and took just a few minutes to warm to my touch.

I continued this light stroking of myself and I must say, it felt good. But there was one thing that sent me in a tailspin. I realized what pleasure my friends had received in practicing this new ritual. As I gently glided my hand up my shaft, the mere touch of my thumb flicking the head of my penis sent shivers up my spine. It felt like tiny fingers massaging my entire body. I felt a pulsating feeling in my hand and realized it was me. I continued this slow motion until I dozed off to sleep.

I awoke the next morning, feeling strangely satisfied and relieved that I had encountered this wonderful experience. That is until I walked down the hallway to the bathroom. Upon pulling my underwear down to release the stream of urine that built up overnight, I noticed something wrong. I was not the size I was before I started masturbating. After attempting to urinate, I stumbled to my mother's room to show her the strange abnormality.

She guided me into my room and closed the door. I quietly removed my underwear for her viewing. I found myself lying to her as she questioned what had happened. I told her in a faint voice that when I woke up, it looked like it did at that moment, swollen and strangely purple. Fearing for my well-being, she made her way immediately to the telephone to call him. She picked up the receiver and dialed the seven-digit emergency number for the same doctor who'd informed me something like this would happen if I masturbated. I panicked. I was scared. I heard my mother explain in explicit detail what my private region looked like. I stood there. Through the receiver, I could hear the chuckles from my doctor. He alerted my mother of my actions and informed her the swelling would eventually go down. He placed her on hold as she directed her questions to me once again. "I'm going to ask you one more time," she said. "What did you do?"

I knew that I couldn't hold back any longer, my secret had been discovered. I shouted as I ran back into my room, "I was playing with myself!" I did not see or speak to my mother for the remainder of the day.

Little did I know, the next step in masturbation was ejaculation. The first time it happened, I was overjoyed at the sensation. Just about every day, I found a reason to touch myself. I enjoyed the thrill of working my dick until the last few seconds before eruption.

As I got better with this newfound joy, I learned to take my little friend to new heights of excitement. I had received a Glow Ball for Christmas. It was nothing more than an inflatable ball with a small insertion for a pen flashlight. It allowed my friends and me to play volleyball at night, as the light illuminated the concrete playground. After tossing and batting it around for hours with my friends, I found new uses for it. If and when I had exhausted the towel I kept hidden under my mattress to clean myself after cumming, I would focus my attention on the Glow Ball and the insertion. It was a perfect fit. I had taught myself enough to hold back when I felt myself about to release. And now, I was sitting across from a thirty-year-old woman, wanting to show her what I had learned and perfected.

She started to caress my inner thigh, resting for a moment before she reached the bottom of my jogging shorts. I had only seen things like this happen in the adult eight-millimeter films my friends' fathers hid in the back of their closets. I knew what would happen next. Without another word spoken between us, she took my hand and guided me instinctively through the dark apartment to her bedroom. It was barely furnished, with a bed in the middle of the room. Because of the lack of electricity, the bedroom window was generously opened to allow brief relief from the rising heat. There was a sheet barely covering the stained mattress as she sat down in front of me. I looked out of the window to see the bright back porch light of my grandma's house. Seeing the light made me nervous and want to bolt from the room. I felt my grandma's eyes staring at me with a disapproving look. As I attempted to leave, she grabbed me about the waist. She must have felt my hesitancy, because she applied a reassuring grip to my hips.

She removed the jogging shorts from my waist, exposing my erection.

Silently she removed her clothes. Taking a page from her direction, I quickly removed the remainder of my summer attire. Even though the air was still, I shivered a little bit from being totally naked before this woman, a woman who had shared herself with many others, including my cousin. She reached for me and gently pulled me on top of her. Visions of the sexual acts I saw performed in those reel films entered my thoughts as I prepared myself for what to do next.

I lay there on top of her and waited for guidance. She took me in her and guided me in. I assumed because she had four kids, there would be a certain amount of looseness and moisture to her opening. What I found was that she was dry and tight. I closed my eyes and replayed the scenes from those movies. I remembered vividly the well-endowed black men thrusting in and out of the women, who seemed to be experiencing much pleasure. I attempted to impersonate to the best of my ability those images at the age of fifteen. I wasn't as blessed with the size of those actors, yet I was a good student of imagery.

I placed her almost anorexic legs around the folds of my arms, resting right where the elbow locked. During this introduction to manhood, I would sneak a peek out of the bedroom window at Grandma's house. Watching the fluorescent light allowed me to think I was the star of my own adult film, viewing the images on screen I attempted to improvise. With my second and third thrust into her used body, I leaned forward to take her nipple into my mouth. She was not a well-blessed woman by any means. Her thin frame and underdeveloped body would have been the envy of today's top models had she taken better care of herself. With her beauty intact, she would have been afforded possibilities of some short-lived regional modeling prospects. The taste of her nipple was not what I imagined. It did not bear the tender sweetness that I thought it would. Her dry lips reached for my neck and bit down. This, for me, was an indication that I was doing something right. I continued forcing myself in, listening to her quiet moans and gasps. Was my performance that great, or was she seeking air from the heat? Whatever the reasons, I felt my body clench as I went in as far as I could. Next thing I knew, it was over.

I turned back around as I entered the backyard gate of Grandma's house to see her image. I could only imagine, at that moment, what my friends would say back home. I would get the high-fives and the thumbs up for fucking a thirty-year-old woman, but the only pat on the back I wanted was from my father.

Before I could celebrate this coming-of-age event with my father, my mother would hear of it first. When I walked into Grandma's kitchen, I knew that I was in trouble. Grandma was on the telephone, long distance with my mother. She was pissed. From what I could gather from the conversation, my mother was on her way to Richmond as soon as she ended her work day the following afternoon. I wore the necklace of love bites engulfing my neck like a badge of honor, but I knew trouble was brewing and she was headed this way.

I watched the clock, counting down to my mother's arrival. She was taking a cab from the local Trailways station and she would be here shortly. When she arrived, I wanted to throw my arms around her neck, but she couldn't stand to look at me. She instructed me to take my ass to bed while she stayed up with Grandma. In my room away from home, behind closed doors, I could hear the wheels turning in my mother's head. Nothing Grandma said or did calmed her. I went to bed with the covers pulled tightly around me, waiting for everything to explode.

And that it did. Saturday morning arrived and at precisely 7:20 a.m. I heard my mother beckon for her appearance. In my most valiant effort for a fifteen-year-old man-child, I pleaded with my mother not to do this. Rage burned deep in her eyes with every step the neighbor made toward the back door. My mother had demanded not only her attendance, but my father's as well. He would be arriving soon, but for now, this played out like an old 45 record, one woman confronting another over one's man.

"What kind of woman would let a fifteen-year-old boy fuck her?" started the first line of this song. This was followed by my mother's chorus, "I would rather have my son fuck his fist, than let him fuck something like you!" I could feel the song reaching its climax, the part that always sends you saying, "You go, girl! Tell her!" As the song reached its high point, I heard it, "You better get the fuck out of here before I fuck you up, you nasty bitch!" And on that note, the song was over.

My mother walked past me as if I wasn't there. Like the great musical divas I had come to admire, she made a grand gesture and walked off stage. Her next performance began when my father rang the doorbell to take his seat for her command performance. She rehashed everything for him with the same fire she had performed earlier with the lady who had just slept with me. "You better handle this boy," she yelled, pointing in my direction.

I sat there waiting for my father to come to my defense. I waited eagerly for once, his approval. This would be the defining moment in our relationship. I had become the man he wanted and he would put my mother in her place. He would forcefully tell her to celebrate my becoming a man. Yes, this is what I had been wanting to cement our relationship. We could now spend our few fleeting moments together in search of pussy. But it never happened. His utterance was simple and to the point. Without as much as a smile or an acknowledgment of this great triumph, my father made one comment to close this tragic musical, "Well, I'm glad it was a girl and not a guy." And it was done. Nothing else to be discussed, nothing else to expect. Before he exited stage right, he pulled out his checkbook to write out the child support check; this way he avoided the postage needed to mail it. I was once again disappointed. I had hoped my father would come to my rescue as I had attempted to aid my one-night stand. But my mother would have none of it. I started to pack my suitcases for the three-hour bus ride back to Baltimore. During the last month or so I had been here, this was the most time my father had spent with me. Once again, he had as in the past let me down. With a quick ruffle of my hair, he left, but all I remembered was the view of him pulling off in his car and me standing there waiting and waiting. For nothing.

My mother and I didn't speak a word on the journey back to Baltimore. It gave me time to think about her reaction about what had happened with my grandma's neighbor and me, but it also allowed me some time to think about my father's reaction. I couldn't read on his face whether he was proud of what I had done. Did he somehow see what was ahead of me based on his comment? I never got the chance to ask, for as soon as he arrived that Saturday morning, he left. I kept replaying my father's statement. It haunts me to this day.

chapter five

I spent the rest of my summer trying to find things to do with myself. I had pissed away all hopes of buying a car for my first day of my junior year. The only things that I could share when I returned to school were my mug-shot learner's permit and the bragging rights to my one-night stand.

I called old friends as the school year grew closer. Some of my friends now had cars, girlfriends and wonderful stories of their summer vacations. My summer paled in comparison. A few of my friends were recent graduates and I wanted to wish them well on their new ventures. Alex, one friend I had contacted, had decided to stay in Baltimore and attend the local community college. Because he had a shit load of brothers and sisters, he took it upon himself to pay for his own tuition. He informed me that he had found a job working the front door of a local bar in the Fells Point community of Baltimore. I had heard him mention the bar's name in conversation with girls in our student government homeroom.

I was the lone person of color in this elitist, self-absorbed classroom. The so-called "who's who" of students were selected specially for this homeroom. The homeroom represented the makeup of the student government, and the bodies represented those of freshmen, sophomores, juniors and seniors. Outside of sharing conversations about the latest Izod clothing line and addressing the "politics" of being popular, it served no other purpose than to give the Tammy Faye Bakker look-a-like adviser an opportunity to wave her hand in the air at pep rallies. She and her jock coach of a husband were the Ken and Barbie of the high school. You couldn't say one's name without including the other. She tolerated me because I spoke up for myself and I tolerated her because she was a figure of authority; otherwise we mixed like oil and water.

Sometimes I wondered who wore the pants in her marriage. Her husband was a pretty likable guy, at times passive, but spending time in his fifty-minute gym class was a hell of a lot better than spending twenty minutes in her homeroom. This is where I met Alex.

He wore arrogance with confidence. With his neatly pressed oxford shirt and matching pants, he glided through the halls every morning with an air of light femininity. Sometimes, I thought he was gliding as he made his way from class to class, ignoring the taunts of the high school jocks. I assumed the phrases of "sissy" and "fag" must have hurt him, but if they did, he never allowed anyone to see him lower his head. For some reason, I admired him. We were similar in some ways, yet very different in others. I, too, held my head high as I walked the halls, but immediately avoided eye contact with anyone who mouthed the word "nigger" in my direction. We were both popular, but for all the wrong reasons.

As Alex and I continued to reminisce about our year together in Barbie's homeroom class, he came up with a bright idea. He extended an invitation for me to visit his place of work and hang out. I always had a good time conversing with him, so I didn't put up much of an argument outside of the fact that I was underage. That was not to be an issue. He tended the door and would gladly let me in. So we planned my trip to Fells Point.

Right about this time, I began to lie to my mother. I was so disappointed and hurt from her recent outburst in dealing with the neighbor woman and me, that I felt a wedge had been driven between the two of us. I found myself making up stories of going with friends to downtown Harborplace to hang out and grab pizza. She was none the wiser. I made sure I made it home before curfew, but this time I had to figure a way to stay out later than usual since I was planning to visit Alex.

I couldn't think up a good enough lie for the night. I would only get better with that over time, so I got dressed and hopped on the Cedonia 5 heading downtown. As I rode the bus that evening, I peered out the window so that I would not miss my stop. I remembered that before heading to Grandma's for the summer, I had dozed off on the bus and wound up in some distant part of Baltimore I had never seen before. While watching the lights, I thought back to my evening with her and the morning my mother confronted her. My heart felt sorry for her. I wanted to strike out at them all for doing what they did to her. I was too young to protect her, but I knew how she felt.

As I located the stop Alex had mentioned, I reached for the bell signaling my desire to exit. As I left the bus, I wondered how my parents would feel about my defiance. *How mad are they going to be?* I didn't care, I was fifteen and I had already begun to smell my piss.

When I rounded the corner, I thought about seeing Alex for the first time since he had graduated. In high school, Alex was everything that I wanted to be. Every morning I looked forward to his latest color-scheme combination. He was also funny. He had a biting sense of humor toward all the jeers he received walking down the school's glass-enclosed hallway toward the cafeteria. If the words of his onlookers bothered him, he never allowed them to see him flinch. He was one of the most popular students in high school for better or worse. Everyone knew of him and his antics. He was also gay—a revelation that everyone knew. I knew by accepting his invitation to his job that I would be going to a gay bar, but I wanted to see him and deep down inside there was a lurking curiosity.

I followed the directions to a tee and found myself staring at the door of the nondescript nightspot. At that moment, my father's words entered my thoughts again: "I'm glad it was a girl and not a guy." Now that I had arrived, I wanted to turn around and head back toward the bus stop to make the last connection. I didn't want to disrespect my father by entering, because I so desperately wanted to be like him, to have his approval. By entering, I would further destroy what little relationship we had. *What would he say now?* I let the thought pass as I stepped aside as the patrons politely excused themselves to enter. For some reason I didn't run away. It was something intoxicating about the music blaring from the inside of the small building. It was also something oddly appealing about the customers sauntering in, smiling and saying "hello" as they passed me. I took a deep breath and entered.

There he was in all his glory—Alex. The outfit was more colorful than I had ever seen. As he had told me on the phone, he was working the door. He kept his promise of free admission as he made his way from his throne to greet me. What a way to live. It's always nice to know high people in low places.

He provided me with one of his air kisses I remembered seeing him use to greet the girls in our production of *The Wizard of Oz*. I was a little bitter that he had beaten me out for the role of Scarecrow in the spring show, but he did a great job. As he showed me around, he decided to drop a bomb on me. He informed me that another former classmate and friend was also in attendance. Knowing what I know now, I realized that Carol was a "fag-hag." She enjoyed the company of homosexuals and she had no problem in admitting this fact. She was very fond of Alex, and even went as far as showing her feelings by dating him. A bit nervous, I allowed Alex to walk me over to her. She reached out to me, grabbing me in a bear hug, and said, "Hey, you." Then she winked, smiled and nodded. It was okay. Without saying another word about my attendance, she silently reassured me that my secret was safe. Over the deafening music and after a couple of turns toward the bar to ensure her drink order was correct, she introduced me to her little group of friends. I stretched my ear to hear all of their names, but the only one that stood out was his. "This is Michael," she yelled. I smiled and extended my hand. In return he did the same.

I watched carefully throughout the course of the night: these men from all walks of life, laughing and enjoying each other's company. I started to loosen up as the evening progressed. It was helped more so by the sips of cheap rum and Coke Carol allowed me to steal from her numerous drinks, but I had my limitations. One guy had asked me to dance and I flat out said, "No." I figured that my mouth and my attitude would get me into trouble, so I opted to chat with the guys Carol had introduced me to earlier that evening. Carol and Michael were on the dance floor, leaving me with a friend of Michael's who was more than cordial. We found ourselves off from the dance floor where I had an opportunity to ask a series of questions I so desperately wanted answers to. I felt like a little boy asking if there were indeed a Santa Claus.

"Are you gay?" was the first question that leapt from my mouth to Michael's friend's ear, with my mouth barely touching the blond hair caressing it. I could see his mind wrapping his thoughts around the question before he answered, "Well, I am bisexual." I shook my head as if to say, *what the fuck does that mean?* Sensing that I didn't understand the answer, he quickly informed me, "I date both guys and girls, but I only sleep with men." I must have still looked puzzled, but I figured I would learn more somewhere down the road.

The night was quickly coming to a close and I faced the dilemma that I hadn't thought about earlier. I knew there were no buses running this late and I certainly didn't have the money to catch a taxi home. I wanted to kick myself as I thought about the possibility of having to call my mother and tell her where I was. Carol saw the fear in my face and placed her arms around me as she offered me a ride home. I sighed. As we were leaving, something strange happened. Michael extended his hand once again and said, "It was a pleasure meeting you, I hope to see you again soon." I don't think I'd said more than five or six words to him the entire evening. I'd spent a great deal of the time talking to his friend and surveying the place. I shrugged it off as we all said good night and I headed back to Lodestone Way.

chapter six

As we neared the intersection of my apartment complex, I began to reflect on the evening. If I were being completely honest with myself, I had a great time. I enjoyed the carefree attitude of the clubbers. But there was one thing that really stood out and it was probably the least significant moment of the evening. They were Michael's parting words to me: "It was a pleasure meeting you, I hope to see you again soon." I felt warm inside from the combination of alcohol and the simple phrase as Carol's car came to a stop in the parking space facing my apartment. I knew once I reached the top of the stairs and placed my key in the door, I was going to get a royal cussing out. But at this moment, I couldn't think of that; the only thing that I wanted to think about was Michael.

My emotional interest in Michael was the first of its kind for me. I remember at the early ages of seven and eight, having sleepovers with my friend Walter. We would always find ourselves wrestling before we went to bed. Even though I had two single beds in my room, he always found his way into the bed I chose, close to the window. As we got older and started to experiment a little more, we found ourselves playing show and tell underneath the covers with a flashlight. This eventually progressed to lying on top of each other, rubbing against the other. But we were kids, we were best friends. Didn't all best friends do that at some point? There was no emotional tie to what we did, just friends exploring.

It was as if I had psychic powers. When I turned the key to enter the apartment I shared with my mother, she began with the "where have you been" questions. I couldn't think of anything to say, I was trying to keep still and focus on looking sober. I remained quiet until she ran out of steam. Before she retired to her bedroom, I was given my first official punishment—no telephone usage for the next twenty-four hours. I followed behind her, closing my door and crawling into bed. I thought once again about the show and tell with my former best friend Walter, and wondered if there was a way Michael and I could play show and tell.

After my twenty-four-hour punishment, I immediately called Carol. I guess she sensed the excitement in my voice and made the suggestion of heading back to Fells Point. I acted as if I really didn't care, but eagerly awaited her arrival in two days. Over the course of those days, we talked more. I acted as if I were genuinely interested in her summer and her plans for college, but in actuality, I wanted to hear more about Michael. She was the bridge between the two of us.

I dropped the casual question, "How do you know him?" She volunteered the information as if she were on a job interview. Freely, she informed me that Michael was her manager at the clothing store where she worked for the summer. She spoke volumes about his interests; he was a theology student who recently had relocated to Baltimore from Kentucky. Throughout the conversation, I heard in her voice her deep admiration and attraction toward him. I wanted to share with her my feelings as well, but friendship was important and she was my ride to see him again. So, I kept my mouth shut.

I looked around for Alex as we entered what I now called my "hot spot." After my investigation, I was informed by Carol that he had a date that evening and would not be working. I was a little disappointed because I wanted to thank him for letting me in the other night. But I could wait to show my gratitude later. After looking around for a bit, I felt unfamiliar arms come up and hug me from behind. It was Michael. I was a bit caught off guard by his generous affection, but I welcomed the closeness of his breath on my neck. He then turned his attention to Carol and motioned for us to join him at the bar. Although I had sipped from Carol's numerous drinks the first night I attended, I had never really had a full mixed drink of my own.

The closest I had come to alcohol was a game of Quarters at a high school Powder Puff afterparty. My high school had a tradition of the freshman class playing the sophomore class in a role-reversal soccer game. Since I was president of my sophomore class, I was elected to head the male cheerleading squad for the sophomores. After our unceremonious loss to the freshman class, we gathered at one of the female players' homes for a celebration party.

I leaned over the shoulders of some of the other male cheerleaders to see what they were watching. They made way for me as I inched closer to see a group of my classmates bouncing quarters off the table to make them land into a glass of beer. One of the guys I had taught to cheer had made room for me next to him. This was his time to teach me the game. Each time the quarter landed in the glass, the glass was passed to me to drink. When I failed to make the quarter in the glass, I was forced to drink. During the hour or so we played, I noticed that I was the only one drinking. The next day at school, I found out it was all a ruse to get the class president drunk since I was so straight-laced.

Now wouldn't they be surprised to see me having my very first full mixed drink of rum and Coke, I thought. The first sip of the drink burned my throat going down. Michael laughed as he lifted my hand again to my mouth to swallow another gulp of the drink. After a few more rum and Cokes, I found my body being taken over by the vibrating speakers. I closed my eyes and swayed to and fro. I was getting into the moment and it felt good. At Carol's urging, she asked me to dance with Michael. I was a bit shocked at the suggestion. This was all happening too fast. Before I could turn down the invitation, the two of them had pulled me onto the dance floor, making me spill my precious concoction. The alcohol had already kicked in and I felt this euphoric feeling overcome me. I danced around with my eyes closed allowing the music to seize hold of me. When I opened them again, Carol was gone. I looked for her, but she had made her way back to the bar to purchase more drinks. But she didn't leave me alone.

Michael was there to take her place. He made his way closer to me as he placed his arms around my neck. He pulled me closer to him. "I like you," he whispered in my ear, with the faint smell of his drink of choice stinging my nose as he pulled back to look me directly in my eyes. As he searched my face for a response, he pressed his body against mine. My mind told me to tell him to stop, but I just wanted to enjoy this moment. As he continued to grind his body into mine, I felt a strange feeling overcome me, a feeling I had only experienced a couple of times at basement birthday parties with girls I slowdragged with. Oh shit! I slowly began to get a hard-on. This time Michael placed both his arms around my neck. I didn't know whether it was due to his enjoyment as well, feeling my hardness rubbing against him, or whether he was attempting to prevent me any embarrassment from my obvious erection.

Whatever it was, who cared? The song had ended and it was time to go. Carol was saying good night to the new bar friends she had made. Michael pulled me to the side to say good night. Or at least I thought it was to say good night. I felt his hot breath in my ear. "I'll give you a ride back to my house and Carol can follow us, if you don't mind," he said with a smile and the most beautiful, piercing blue eyes that seemed to plead with my confused mind.

Before I knew it, we were entering Michael's studio apartment with Carol in tow. I searched for a place to sit down, gather my thoughts and sober up from the drinks I'd consumed. The apartment was small, yet large enough to hold a queen-sized bed, some living room furniture for entertaining, and a small dining set. I stumbled toward the rocking chair placed next to Michael's bed. It allowed me to see the television set off in the corner. Carol tried to get my attention with her stories of her meeting hot sexy men at the bar, while I focused on the alcohol sloshing around in my empty stomach. I wanted to continue to play the grownup this evening, as I accepted a glass of wine from Michael. Carol elected to skip this round of drinks, as she decided to call it an evening.

As Michael walked Carol to the door, I took that as my cue to interrupt the union between my ass and the comfortable rocker. I managed to pull myself up and follow the two of them to the door to make my exit with Carol. "I can give you a ride home if you would like to stay," Michael urged in his seductive way. Carol and I made eye contact with each other and I assured her I would be okay. I sensed a bit of anger in her eyes as she quickly headed out the door. I couldn't turn Michael down. As I looked deeper into his deep ocean-blue eyes, I somehow felt they had placed a spell on me the earlier part of the evening and they were continuing their seduction.

Michael closed the door behind Carol and made his way over to the waist-high refrigerator. He poured me another glass of wine. I drank it like a thirsty man, partly parched, partly nerves. Outside of the noise coming from the television, you could hear a pin drop. I felt a bit awkward and attempted to break the silence. Through the slurring, I managed to get out, "You know Carol likes you?" He looked back at me as he poured yet another glass of wine. He smiled that smile again, looking directly at me. I could not turn away as he said, "I know she does, but she doesn't turn me on. You, on the other hand, do." As he said that, he made his way over to the edge of the bed, right beside the rocking chair. He poured me another glass of wine. I gulped the contents of the glass, hoping that he could not sense my fear. He knelt before me and removed the glass from my trembling hand. He said softly, "Do not be nervous. If you want me to stop, I will."

I didn't want him to. He placed his soft hands around my face. He cupped my cheeks the way a mother embraces her newborn. He leaned toward me and gently kissed me. My head started to swim again. The wine, the television and the kiss were beginning to play mind games with me. At the same time, the feeling I'd experienced with Michael on the dance floor presented itself once again.

As Michael pulled away, I kept my eyes closed, savoring the taste of his kiss. "Are you okay?" was his next question, but before I could answer, he kissed me once again. This time the kiss lasted longer. Michael opened my mouth with his skillful tongue and continued to kiss me the way a former girlfriend taught me how. Only at that moment did I realize that with my eyes closed, I really couldn't tell whether it was her or Michael. I didn't care. I was with someone who said they liked me and wanted me. That's all that mattered.

I continued to lose myself in what I thought was a forbidden moment. I began to feel somewhat uncomfortable; not because I was kissing Michael, but because I didn't know what to do next. I had limited experience with women and this was all new to me. I knew nothing about being with a man or if it were possible to make love to a man. Since we were both born with the same organs, was it possible to experience what I'd had with her? The answers to those bothersome questions were soon revealed by my new teacher.

Michael continued to explore my mouth with his tongue. At the same time, he removed my shirt. We parted for a moment, my lips searching for his, as he removed my shoes. He made his way back to my neck. He pressed his lips softly into the side of my neck, as he took his tongue and licked my ear. His fingers fumbled for a moment at my belt and the zipper of my pants. He removed my pants, leaving me there exposed. I was somewhat self-conscious of my body. At fifteen, puberty wasn't quite over. I sat there as he explored my underdeveloped body and man-sized hard-on.

Sitting there in my plain white-cotton Fruit of the Looms, Michael stood above me. I grabbed the remains of the glass of wine, quenching my thirst for his kiss once again. He removed his clothing, stripping down to a form-fitting pair of blue-and-white-striped bikini briefs. I thought to myself, *I need to buy some new underwear, or better yet, ask my mother to pick some up for my upcoming birthday*. Michael removed the glass from my hand once again. He reached for my other hand and guided me the few steps to his bed. I was not prepared for what happened next, but I anxiously waited for it to resume.

He picked up where he'd left off. He laid me on the bed. His tongue continued to dance wildly in my mouth. His hands began to caress my shivering body. His exploration this time led to the inside of my underwear. He removed my briefs by the band. I watched as he raised himself up on his knees and removed his. His hot mouth pecked away at my chest in a downward spiral. Slowly he engulfed my nipple in his mouth as I had done with her only a few weeks earlier. He continued lower, resting his face against the growing treasure trail that led to my throbbing dick. He placed his hands around me. From the lighting of the television, I watched as his eyes slowly disappeared as he placed his warm and welcoming mouth on my head.

As the warmth of his mouth and saliva covered me, he slowly took more of me into his mouth. I started to wriggle at the sensation. For the first time in my life, I was receiving a blowjob. I always knew that I would get one at some point in my life, but never did I think it would be from another man. What a wonderful feeling. I wanted to go out the next day and tell my friends I had received my first blowjob. How could I tell them without revealing that the doer of the deed was another man, a man of twenty-five. As I pondered the question, Michael returned to me to claim his position next to me. He now had a bottle in his hand.

"I want you to try this while I continue to do what I am doing," he said. He instructed me to hold the vial to my nostril and inhale, while pinching closed the other nostril. Once I inhaled, I was to hold my breath for a few moments and then exhale. I questioned the contents of the bottle. He smiled and educated me of its contents. "Poppers," he said. "It will relax you and make you feel good." I was assured that it would not cause any harm. As with my father, I didn't want to disappoint Michael. Little did I know at that time, the contents of this little bottle contained embalming fluid. As I got older and continued its use, I found out it causes a loss of brain cells. That night I lost quite a few.

I did as I was instructed. Michael made his way back down to my dick. When he took me once again in his mouth, the feeling forced me to exhale the contents before I was ready. It didn't matter. Suddenly my mind started to fly. It took every ounce of control left in my body to comprehend where I was and what I was doing. I felt like I was experiencing this incredible out-of-body experience, hovering over Michael and my physical self watching this beautiful moment. The embalming fluid had reached my brain cells and had begun stimulating my entire body. I looked down at Michael's head making a slow up-and-down movement. I rested my head on the pillow and drifted off into a world I had never been to.

I attempted in vain to gather myself from the poppers. As I took another breath, Michael stopped sucking me and forced his tongue deep in my mouth. His hand was still working on my dick, but this time I felt what appeared to be a sticky substance being applied to it. Michael stopped kissing me and told me to take another whiff of the poppers. He then took a sniff of its contents. My heart started to race again. I began to float once more, only to be met halfway. Michael had lowered himself onto me. I wanted to bust from the pleasure I was experiencing. I raised myself up on my elbows, only to have Michael slide his sticky hand across my chest, forcing me back down. I couldn't see his face because his head was hanging down. When he finally looked up at me, there was a silent pleading in his baby blues. "Go slow," he whispered.

Once again as I did with Grandma's neighbor, I quickly replayed those movies I had watched on the walls of my buddy's basement, attempting to remember what positions brought pleasure to the women in those silent films. Michael continued to slide up and down me. He reached for the bottle once again, first he inhaled and then he grabbed the back of my head, holding it at the nape allowing me to inhale as well. He eventually became adjusted to me being inside of him. I decided to take the lead from this point. I gently rolled him over onto his back.

I continued the gliding in and out that he'd initially started. His ass reminded me of the tightness of her opening, but he was far more lubricated. The feeling began to take over me as I increased the speed and consistency of fucking him. A slight moan escaped from his mouth and I stopped. Was I hurting him? He assured me that I wasn't and encouraged me to continue.

After receiving the go-ahead, I proceeded to take him in every position I could remember. After a few more strokes on his back, I turned him over and took him from behind, doggy style. The tightness of his sphincter muscle massaged my dick as I increased the movement.

The pressure of my body forced Michael onto his stomach. In perfect pushup form and at my own discretion, I found myself creating my own movements. Hearing his whispers of "yes," I figured from certain angles, which movements increased not only his pleasure, but intensified mine as well. I lowered myself toward his neck, motioning his head to face the side so that I could kiss him. He willingly obliged. In this position, although I was no John Holmes, I realized that I had control over the situation and it allowed for deeper penetration.

Suddenly, I felt my body shudder. *Oh God!* My arms started to give way as everything in my body made its way to my dick. I fell into Michael one last time, as I felt it, the explosion that had been building since that first dance. I thrust myself deeper into him, collapsing in exhaustion on his back. The suction from his ass made me quiver as I released the final drops of cum inside him. My once-hard dick was now soft and sore from this workout. Feeling like I had done this so many times before, I gently kissed the back of his neck once again, closed my eyes, and whispered, "I love you."

I slept like a baby. The only thing that roused me from my sleep was Michael preparing for work. Because I still had a couple of weeks before school started, I was in no big rush to greet the morning sunshine. The sunlight beamed through the window, forcing me to close my eyes. I basked in the moment that the previous night had brought forth in my life. I propped myself up on my side to watch Michael finish tying his tie. As he scurried about, I looked around searching for my clothes. Over in one corner were my socks and shoes, the other corner, my pants and right at the foot of the bed were my briefs. I reached for the underwear to get dressed so that I could exit with him and make my way home. He leaned over to me and instructed me to lie back down and get some sleep. He would be back later to take me home. I couldn't think of a reason why I would rush home to the ass whipping awaiting me, so I grabbed the pillow and held it the way I did him. He kissed me gently, with the fresh taste of toothpaste, and smiled as he closed the door behind him. I closed my eyes once again and for the next few hours, slept peacefully waiting for Michael's return.

I was awakened later that afternoon by Michael crawling into bed with me. He had closed the blinds before he left and the room was filled with the light we generated. We held each other and kissed. It didn't bother him that I still had the lingering taste of rum on my breath. He kissed me deeply. I was still naked and noticed that as he got under the covers with me, so was he. We made love once again. We fell asleep briefly after our second passionate interlude. It was time to interrupt this dream for a moment and face my reality.

I noticed the landmarks heading toward my house from Michael's place. We listened to the songs playing on the radio and silently communicated.

As he veered into the parking lot, he said good-bye with the promise of calling me later that evening. I was still tired from our second round and needed an additional nap. Luckily my mother would not be home from work for another couple of hours. I made my way to my back bedroom and stacked the 45's onto the record player that I wanted to hear. That was the summer of 1984 when lyrics actually spoke to the heart. I placed Peabo Bryson's "If Ever You're in My Arms Again" first, followed by The Cars' "Drive." Closing out this "Quiet Storm" evening drive was Bananarama's "Cruel Summer." I closed my eyes, listening to Peabo croon and reminiscing of Michael.

I never heard the phone ring that evening. This was way before the days of my mother purchasing an answering machine. Instead of the ringing, I only heard my mother's voice.

On and on she went about how defiant I had become, throwing in my face the lying and the evening I'd spent with the lady she despised. She informed me how disappointed she was in my behavior and the threats of calling my father if I didn't get my act together. She followed it up with the threat of sending me to live with him. I knew this wasn't going to happen. Hell, to him, I barely existed. As I figured she would, she reminded me once again of that piss smell I was starting to develop, but all I could smell were the poppers from the night with Michael. Even while she was ripping me a new asshole, the telephone never rang.

Twenty-four hours had passed and there was no call from Michael. Although we didn't own an answering machine, Michael did. I called. I left a message. I called back and left another message. I tried later and left a message. It was only his voice repeating the same refrain, "Leave a message, I'll get back to you." *Beep.*

Dammit! If I had only worked with my uncle that summer, I could have driven to Michael's house, instead of managing to avoid the beeping cars on Pulaski Highway on my ten-speed. I would stop on occasion as I remembered the storefronts and at which highway motels we made right turns. I found myself in his apartment complex, breathing heavily from the fear of being hit by one of the big-rig trucks. I was now at the entrance to the den of paradise I had just left a couple of days earlier. I imagined that when I entered, he would have the lights turned down low, my glass filled with wine, and we would make love once again to make up for the lost time we had missed. I knocked on the door. I searched for the blue eyes of Michael, but the eyes that greeted me were not his.

My heart started to race more. I looked around for Michael as I was invited in. Without a word spoken between the two of us, this doorman walked out and closed the front door behind him. "I tried calling you," Michael said, breaking the silence. I stumbled over my words, telling him that I went back to sleep after he had dropped me off. He turned his back toward me, looking in the three-quarter-length mirror attached to the wall to make sure he didn't miss any of the loops while putting on his belt. I asked what was going on, feeling coldness in the air from him.

His eyes never met mine as he said, "I think you are a good kid." He brushed his shirt off and darted his head in my direction. "But I could never really have anything with you." My heart dropped. "You're only fifteen years old; I'm twenty-five, where could I possibly take you? What could we possibly do?"

I attempted to spit out, "But we made love," but the words got lost in the lump forming in my throat. On cue, the doorman entered, leaving the door open for me to exit. He went and stood next to Michael as Michael said, "Good-bye."

I couldn't see through the tears streaming down my face. I was once again on my bike pedaling, pedaling hard, and running away from this nightmare. I managed somehow to wipe my face so that I could see enough of the oncoming traffic without losing my balance. But the tears that I soon wiped away were replaced by many others. To avoid any traffic accidents, I cut down the dark winding road, heading to a former classmate's house. Unlike me, he had purchased a car and was out with his girlfriend when I arrived.

His father, Mr. Peters, was an aspiring bodybuilder and greeted my tears with a concerned look. I couldn't begin to tell Mr. Peters through my tears what I was feeling and he didn't bother to ask. He informed his wife that he would return after taking me home. He placed my bike in the trunk of his car and we sat quietly as I stifled my sobs. We pulled into the parking of the apartment complex.

As I reached for the handle to exit and thank him, I felt Mr. Peters' hand on my shoulder. "What's wrong, son?" he asked, searching for the answers that led to the tears flowing down my cheeks. I was touched by his genuine interest and this too caused more tears. I had known Mr. Peters about five years and my father most of my life, and yet for the first time, a man outside of my father wanted to know what was bothering me.

Mr. Peters gave me what I needed that night, what I had wanted from my own father. Feeling the warmth of his touch, I blurted out the events of the night with Michael. I informed Mr. Peters that I might be gay. He looked at me. His face comforted me as he said, "It doesn't matter. I'm just glad my son has a friend like you." For the first time in fifteen years, I was validated. Someone told me it was okay to be me. A white man, the father of a high school friend, who only knew me through his son, had told me it was okay. I was touched by his sincerity, but in the back of my mind, I wished that the validation had come from my own father. I thanked Mr. Peters for the ride as he helped me retrieve my bike from the trunk. He told me to hang in there before he headed home. I watched as the taillights signaled to make a left turn and I wished at that moment that he were my father.

≈

My sixteenth birthday was approaching. I had received the birthday card from my father that was signed, not by him, but by Della. Nothing extra in the monthly support check, but it was sent close to the time of my upcoming birthday, with the thought of killing two birds with one stone. By this time, I had sunk into a deep depression since that night at Michael's. I found myself confined to my bedroom listening to my own formatted radio station. Rather than listen to the lyrics of Peabo's reassurance to a former love of his desire to love her much better, I flipped the 45 over to discover his lover's lament:

"What I need is time, to get over loving you. In my mind, I don't know what I'm gonna do."

In the past, my mother had been able to place a smile on my face at any given moment. She could turn my frown upside-down, but this time there was nothing in her bag of tricks. We chatted briefly after she would arrive home from work and I would excuse myself to my room, close the door, and spend my nights with Peabo.

Grandma's birthday card had arrived in the mail two days before my birthday. By this time, school had started and I had nothing to share or show for my summer. Although it was good to see old friends, I would never be the same since the turn of events that summer. I was happy to see that she had sent cash and not a check or money order. I didn't have to wait until my mother cashed the check to reap the benefits of her birthday gift. After that last night with Michael and adjusting to the beginning of my junior year in high school, I had been wallowing in this pit of hell. I came to the conclusion that there was nothing I could do about it. He wasn't coming back and I had to move on.

I wanted to celebrate my birthday with someone special, so I decided to take "me" out for the evening. I had finally been given permission by my mother to wear jeans. This was a milestone for me, since my father was always opposed to me wearing them. I took the newly purchased jeans from the closet and ironed them the way I had seen my mother do it. Back then, a crease in your jeans had to be sharp. I sprayed some water on the black dress shirt with the burgundy collar I had selected to go with my neatly pressed pants. I reached for the knitted necktie to complement the shirt. I tied it with my eyes closed, remembering how my mother's ex-boyfriend had walked me through the steps. I took an old damp cloth and polished my ankle-high cowboy boots to a high gloss. I added the final touch, when I reached for the beige Members Only jacket to cement the deal. I walked out the door with the birthday money Grandma had sent and headed to the corner bus stop.

Once again, I boarded the Cedonia 5, destination Fells Point. I decided on the ride down that I would avoid the spot where I'd met Michael. It was too painful at this time to see him again. I assumed the next time I would see him, he would be with the doorman who was closer to his age and I couldn't handle that. I opted for the bar next door to the Heartbreak Hotel. I adjusted my jacket and entered.

Just like the Heartbreak Hotel, the music was blaring, competing for the discreet patrons walking by. The gentleman at the door smiled and waved me in, directing me to the dance floor. I stood there drinking in my new surroundings. I was a half hour away from sixteen and I was alone.

I found an empty spot against the wall, where I took up temporary residence. They all walked by: blonds, brunettes, redheads. Some had blue eyes, brown eyes, green eyes, and some even possessed the haunting gray eyes. A few asked me to dance, others asked if they could by me a drink. My Southern upbringing came out in the form of polite thank-yous and no-thank-yous. But one blond-haired, blue-eyed combination later caught my attention.

In the eighties, he could have been the featured face on any number of the high-glossy teen publications targeting young girls. He was the All-American boy. His hair was sandy-blond, slightly tousled, as if you could really make a determination in the dimly lit club. He wore second-skin jeans and a T-shirt, prominently displaying his muscular chest, stretching the logo that spread across it.

I looked away from him as he directed his glance toward me. He made his way over and occupied the vacant spot beside me. I managed to move slightly to give him and his chest more room. He smiled. I found myself looking at him and returning the smile. This time I had no one to protect me, there were no familiar faces to run to or seek for guidance. I thought of situations I had been in at high school dances. If I wanted to dance with the pretty girl in the crowd, I had to ask. Now I was standing next to the pretty boy and I wanted him. I placed myself back in the high school cafeteria and leaned in for the kill. He nodded as he led me to the dance floor, his chest finding a spot for the two of us on the crowded floor.

We danced together for two songs and quickly exited the dance floor when it became flooded by other patrons. He extended his hand and introduced himself and I returned the favor. Over the loud music, I deciphered his next question regarding my age. I looked at my watch and announced that in a matter of minutes I would be turning sixteen. He smiled and wished me a happy birthday. Our heads continued to bob to the music and he turned to face me.

"Is this new to you?" he said, trying to find the answers. I shook my head to the rhythm of the music and nodded. He looked me dead in the eyes as Michael had just a few short weeks earlier. I didn't feel the same passion coming from him as Michael's arms gathering around my neck the first time we danced. There was concern. He looked down for a moment before he faced me again. "Before you become really involved with this, really think about it." I searched his eyes for unsettling answers. He continued, "It's a really hard lifestyle." And with that and a final birthday wish, he walked away. I never saw him again. I was confused by his statement. I didn't know what to make of it. I allowed the echo of his voice to play over and over in my head. Before I realized it, I looked at my watch again. I smiled a sad smile and wished myself a happy birthday.

I looked around for someone else to celebrate my birthday. Everyone seemed to have coupled off and was enjoying their own rites of passage. Right before I had given up all hopes of dancing again, I spotted a guy at the bar. Every time I looked in his direction, he smiled. This was the beginning of many cat-and-mouse games with him during the evening. The last time I went to look in his direction, I noticed that he was no longer at the bar. He was beginning to make his way over to me. As he smiled, I noticed the braces on his teeth. He extended his hand and asked if he could have this dance. We made our way to the crowded dance floor, eager to get one or two more dances in before the voice of "last call" reverberated throughout the club.

I had lost track of time. I had to stop doing this. I knew my mother would pitch a bitch yet again when I arrived home. Only knowing this man for a brief moment, I asked him for a ride. Since he was heading that direction, he said okay. His name was Ken.

During the ride to my apartment, I learned a little more about him. He revealed that he was a recent graduate of a rival high school. As we talked, I took notice of his looks. He was cute in what we call today, a nerdy kind of way. We continued to make our way through the empty streets of Baltimore before he decided to take the conversation in a different direction—my sexual history.

I told him of my limited experience and shared with him my heartbreak over Michael. He made it clear that he was interested in me and wanted to explore something more. Before we arrived at my apartment, Ken found a secluded spot only a few blocks away and provided me with my second-ever blowjob.

We were sitting in the parking lot and he asked for my phone number. I presumed he would probably do the same thing as Michael and not call. I didn't put much stock in his interest as I scribbled my number. I closed the door and thanked him for the ride, knowing good and damn well that he was not going to call. As I turned to enter the apartment building, I looked up and saw my mother peering out the window. I climbed the stairs, turned the key and there she was was.

"Where the fuck have you been?" slapped me in the back of my head as I closed the door and locked it. I didn't answer. This summer had taught me how to lie without giving away the fact that I was lying. But sometimes silence did cover my ass. I managed a feeble excuse of meeting friends from school downtown at Harborplace to celebrate my birthday; at least it sounded good to me. I hoped that she bought that. My mother stubbed her cigarette butt in the overflowing ashtray and got up. I felt myself back up. As long as I could remember, my mother had never spanked me or hit me, but because of everything I had done over the last few months, I feared the long-awaited ass whipping.

"Don't pull this shit again, boy," followed me down the hallway as I made my way to my bedroom. I'm telling you, the tone in which it was delivered, put the fear of Mom in me. I didn't do it for a while. That is until Ken called.

After a few weeks and numerous calls, at the age of sixteen I had my first boyfriend. Our time was limited to getting together after I got out of school. Ken would pick me up sometimes and we would spend a couple of hours riding around, just talking. It was nice to have someone to talk to about the feelings that were beginning to take over my day-to-day thoughts. On rare occasions, we were able to find hidden spots in the area to explore each other.

I found myself spending more time with Ken and less time and thought on school. I didn't want to go to school because I thought my classmates would figure out what was going on. So I started cutting school. I would leave home the same time as my mother and wait for her to board the bus to work. Once the bus was out of sight, I would go back home. Sometimes if he wasn't working, Ken would stop by, other times I would sit there listening to my records.

I started to feel guilty about this secret I was hiding. I felt a large boot on my chest preventing me from rising to the person I always wanted to be and knew that I could be. Any other time I could share with my mother what I was feeling and she would offer kind words of support and encouragement. But for some reason, I couldn't go to her this time. I had not heard from Alex and Carol since school had started and there was no indication that I would ever speak to Michael again. Ken was not only my boyfriend, but he became my therapist, confidant and sounding board. The guilt of discovering and living with the fact that I was now gay started to consume me. My grades were suffering in school from sneaking around with Ken and playing hooky. I felt the need deep within to be myself, but up until this point, I had been everything everybody else wanted me to be. I couldn't handle it. I needed to do something. I decided to run away.

One Friday morning, I sat down at home and wrote two letters. One was to the young lady at school, our junior class vice president. In her letter, I expressed a desire to want to kill myself, without telling her why; and from the guilt that I was carrying inside, I so wanted to die. The letter to my mother informed her that I wanted to get away. I used the excuse of school pressure for my running away from it all. With the help of Ken, I purchased a one-way ticket to Richmond to visit Grandma.

Of course, when I arrived at Grandma's I called my mother to let her know I was okay. She felt better knowing I was safe, but immediately sent me a ticket to return home. I still had school to think about. I returned that Sunday evening, but not before talking to my cousin.

Theresa was exactly seven months and one day older than me. Growing up, she never let me forget this one simple fact. Four of us were raised together like siblings, including her brother, Andrew, and our youngest cousin, Tammy. Although we had different parents, we were as tight as any other set of siblings. We did everything together. So I believed in my head that this bond, this connection we shared, would allow me to share with her the drama that I was going through, the reasons why I was running away, even if I didn't go any further than Grandma's house.

We sat together on her bed facing each other. I mulled over what I would say, but it somehow just came out. I shared with Theresa that I liked boys. I even shared with her the story of Ken. During the years that we'd grown up together, we'd had our battles as all cousins do, but because of the love we shared as family, we'd always found a way to forgive and forget—but not this time. She looked at me with disgust during the moment I needed reassurance and love.

She was raised Catholic. With her deep religious upbringing and views, she expressed hurt and disappointment in me. Her disappointment in me was not as bad as the lies I told myself and others to hide what I was truly feeling and the discovery of who I truly was. Nor was it as bad as what faced me when I returned to school after trusting someone I thought was a friend.

Things only got worse. I returned to school after my getaway. I walked into homeroom and took my seat. There was a different vibe I felt. It was a bit unsettling. During the chatter of conversation, a voice from the PA system announced to everyone in the class that my presence was requested in the guidance counselor's office. As my homeroom teacher instructed me to head to the office, I heard the *oohs* and *ahhs* from my fellow classmates. I turned my head toward the vice president and she looked away. My secret was no longer a secret.

I sat in the lobby of Mr. Ralston's office waiting for the other shoe to drop in my life. He had been my former counselor in junior high school and we had a longstanding relationship. I found him to be a fair man. I was happy to hear that he was promoted to the guidance department of my high school. He was the one and only constant male figure in my life at the time, so I was happy that when I moved to high school, he was there with me. The secretary escorted me into his office; sitting opposite him was my mother and what my eyes could make out on his desk—the letter.

The young lady who would eventually assume my role as class president had taken it upon herself to turn over the letter to our homeroom teacher. She, in turn, forwarded it to Mr. Ralston. After careful review of the letter's contents, the school system determined it was in the best interest of all parties involved that I be enrolled in an acute psychiatric program due to the suicidal thoughts I had revealed. I had shared with this bitch, without revealing my newfound sexuality, that I was having difficulty dealing with certain aspects of my life. My words had gotten me into trouble. Little did I know that would be the last day I would ever see that high school. This was a place where I had made many accomplishments, broken color barriers and established a name for myself. All that remained of my legacy were the whispers among the students I had called friends.

I cried as we headed toward the program that would house me for the next two weeks. The doctors greeted the three of us: my mother, Mr. Ralston and me. Both my mother and Mr. Ralston were leaving me in the hospital. I cried, asking my mother to take me with her. I saw the hurt in her eyes as the nurse escorted the two of them from the locked facility. My eyes burned from the strain of tears, pleading, "Please, Mom, don't leave me." Mr. Ralston placed his arms around my mother for comfort as her tears began to fall. I heard the door lock and they were gone.

Over the next two weeks of dealing with curfews and the door being locked at precisely nine p.m., I was informed that the school system had discovered that my correct address placed me in the vicinity of Baltimore City Public Schools and not that of Baltimore County. Because of location, I would never attend another county school. However, that was the least of my worries. For now the numerous doctors assigned to me wanted to delve into the root of my desire to kill myself. They all believed that I was a bright and articulate young man. I had everything going for me, so why would I want to take away something so precious?

It took me a while to open up to anyone on the floor. I was the youngest person in this looney bin. The closest person in age was thirty-two. I had no one to talk to except for the interns doing their rounds to make their required psych credits. When I finally found my voice to speak, I revealed what was troubling me most. I shared with the interns and doctors, individually and collectively, my attraction to boys.

I was never ostracized for what I was feeling, nor was I encouraged. The solution in the eyes of the doctors was family counseling. To this day, I don't know what was shared with my mother, or what she shared with my father, but he drove three hours to attend the first of many sessions.

I was assured that my conversations with the staff were confidential. So when the family sessions began, I failed to bring up the attraction I was feeling to my mother and father. I focused more on the pressures I encountered being black and not being accepted by my black and white peers alike. Yeah, that was it. I was a misplaced black kid in a community of white folks who were friends by day and bitter enemies by the time the school day was out. Even worse, the feelings I felt from my black friends who criticized me for doing "white things" at school. That worked for a while, but as doctors always do, they dug deeper.

My parents and I sat there, being observed via a two-way mirror by medical students like guinea pigs. I started to peel back the layers of emotions and discuss the relationship, or lack of relationship, I had with my father. I didn't want to upset or offend him so I avoided eye contact. I just wanted so much his love and approval. My words must have triggered something deep in my father; either that or his nervousness he felt from the peering eyes he could not see.

My father began to cry. *What the fuck is he crying for*, I thought. *I'm the one dealing with all of this. He was only here because my mother told him to get his ass here, fast, quick and in a hurry.* This was a breakthrough, but for who? Certainly not me. I was still carrying a heavy burden on my heart. But it worked. My doctors and parents agreed that I was okay and ready to go home. Yes, I was going home, but not to the apartment I called home.

Two days before my discharge, my father returned to Richmond. I was informed by my mother during my final session with her that I would be returning to Richmond. My parents, rather my mother, demanded that my father step up and take an active role in my life and my rearing. She felt I needed a male figure in my life. My father would assume the role of raising me until my mother moved back to Richmond to be with me. He had gotten away the last few years with the monthly support check and none of the day-to-day shit I had put my mother through. It was now his time. With his other kids, who were now adults, and including me, he had an offhand approach to raising us. I left the hospital after two weeks and to me nothing had been accomplished. I had suppressed my feelings and attraction to men to satisfy my parents. Nothing was discussed in our family sessions about me being gay. To my parents, I was just a teenage boy who needed male guidance. I now had to deal with the thought of returning to Richmond.

I didn't have any say-so in the decision. When I arrived at our two-bedroom apartment, my belongings had been neatly laid out and folded for packing. My mother sat me down and promised me everything would be okay. I would only be staying with my father for a couple of months until she moved back. The decision was made. With reluctance, she allowed me to see my friends one last time before the move.

The first person I contacted was Ken. We spent one last moment together saying so long to each other. We promised that we would keep in contact, but I knew this was good-bye.

My few high school friends who were informed that I wasn't returning invited me to a keg party. I didn't shed tears that Saturday night at the party because I knew at any moment I was going to wake up from this bad dream. When I did awake that Sunday morning, I found myself groggy, with a throbbing headache. The taste of celebratory cigars and cigarettes deadened my taste buds. I took the longest shower to sober up from the endless cups of cheap beer from the night before. I snapped back to my reality. In a short time, my father would be arriving to take me to my new home. Before his arrival, I continued to beg my mother to let me stay. I promised that I would be a good boy. I promised I wouldn't stay out late anymore. I pleaded with her to let me stay. My pleading and her packing were interrupted by a knock at the door.

There smiling was my father and his wife, Della. They entered and made their way to the kitchen table that was alongside the living room. For the next half hour, my new parents assured my mother I was in good hands and everything would be all right. Della had spent the last few days preparing for my arrival by setting up my room, and her granddaughter would make sure I found my way around my new school.

My father called me over to him from the sofa and ruffled my hair. He laughed. "Looks like someone had a rough night." I tried to smile but I couldn't. I was hurting inside and no one cared. I knew I had no control over the situation. However, they did allow me one request.

I asked my father if I could visit two of my friends before we departed. He agreed. I could tell by the look on Della's face, she was not happy about this decision. Under further scrutiny, I could feel she was not pleased with the idea of me moving in with her and my father. Her actions clearly showed she did not want to be there as she half-heartedly nodded in agreement.

My mother stayed behind to finish packing as the three of us headed out the door. My first stop was my old pal Russ, who came to see me while I was in the psych ward. The last time I saw him prior to this moment, he was leaving the hospital ward upset. He gave me a hug. Although we'd had a rough time of it when we first met, he was now one of my dearest friends. He attempted to show me in our short friendship it was okay to cry, to let someone know you were hurting. He was one of the few men I would hug in life and know there was love there. He expected nothing in return; unlike the others to follow. I would certainly miss him.

Our next and final stop was the Miller household. When I first moved to Baltimore, the Millers became my extended family. I had attended school with the youngest sister. I said my good-byes and hugged Ms. Barbara, my second mother. I promised her that I would keep in contact with her and the family and that I would do my best to be good. Of all the promises I made in life that was one I tried to keep.

As we hopped in the car, I presumed the next stop would be the apartment, but Della wanted to take advantage of this opportunity and go to Harborplace. I knew she had an ulterior motive for coming with my father. She could not give a flying fuck about me. I wanted to go back and lie down for a moment and sleep off the beer, but she walked my father and me up and down Harborplace so she could purchase a few trinkets.

We finally made it back to the apartment and my bags were packed and waiting at the door. My mother and my new parents sat down for a few more minutes to go over last-minute details. The history between the three had been a turbulent one. My mother was pregnant with me when my father married Della. My mother only found out after receiving a call from his sister crying. She informed my mother that "Lil' Joe" had gotten married. Through the hurt and betrayal, my mother maintained a relationship with him for my sake. But there was no love lost between her and Della.

Della felt threatened by my mother and the other mothers of the kids who called him Joe, not Dad. After my birth, my mother mailed my father baby pictures of me, pictures that he never saw. They were returned cut in half with a note reading, "Keep your bastard son." She used my skin complexion to question the validity of Joe being my father. She determined with her armchair medical degree, that because of my skin complexion, the white store manager where my mother was employed was indeed my true father. So you see, there was some history there. And now she was stuck with the burden of playing surrogate mother to the bastard child of her husband.

The time had come. The afternoon sunlight was slipping away from us and it was time to hit the highway. I began to cry uncontrollably. I didn't want to go. I didn't want to leave my mother. I silently made promises through my tears to God; I would give up this gay life if He allowed me to stay with my mother. I cried and begged her to let me stay as she hugged me one last time. I felt her tears hit the back of my neck as she kissed me good-bye. I pleaded my case again to my father as he ushered me into the car. I saw Della shake my mother's hand and mouth to her, "He'll be okay." I turned my body to look out the rear window, still crying as we pulled out of the parking lot. My mother's hand was around her mouth as she continued to cry, no one there to offer her support. Her image grew smaller and smaller as we turned to hit the main road, until she disappeared from sight. I turned toward my father asking him to take me back; I didn't want to go. But my pleading fell on deaf ears. We made our way to Interstate 95 South and I cried until we arrived in Richmond three hours later.

chapter seven

Dusk began to set in as we pulled up to the yellow-and-brown small frame house I would now call home. It was a small two-bedroom rancher my father had purchased when he and Della married. I had been to this place several times in my youth. Because it was only Della and my father, the second bedroom had been converted into a makeshift den. When visiting, Della did not allow me to sit in the neatly decorated living room. That room was reserved for special people, like her four adult kids, her grandkids, or special guests. To her I was none of the above. I was only allowed to walk through the showpiece as I made my way to the back den.

In the past when I visited, Della's youngest son stayed in the attic. It had been converted into a bedroom to accommodate him until he moved in with his older brother. The den's pullout sofa served as my bed during the few sleepovers I'd had here. As I walked into the house, I presumed that the den had been transformed into my new bedroom. After helping my father unload my suitcases and grabbing something quick to eat, I called my mother. Through the sobs, she told me it was only temporary. She would call me later during the week to check on me. I could hear her voice tremble as she instructed me to behave. Before she hung up the phone she reminded me she loved me.

My father told me to take a shower and prepare something to wear to school the following day. Between the time he left Baltimore to return home, he had enrolled me in the high school where Della's granddaughter attended.

Before I settled on an outfit to wear, he sat there to provide his fashion knowledge. Here I was sixteen and yet my father still controlled what he thought I should wear. For the first week of school, he would not allow me to wear the jeans my mother had purchased for me. I did as I was told.

I took a shower, washing off the tears from the three-hour drive and allowing my body to relax just a bit. After the shower, I entered the den in search of my suitcase. I looked around and found nothing. My father called me into the kitchen and pulled the steps down to the attic. He carefully showed my how to pull the cord on the ceiling door to lower the steps to my new room.

Because the latch that secured the folding stairs was worn, I was shown how to place my hands on the latch, holding it in place and lowering the steps to rest on the stool located near the washing machine. If I was too quick at releasing the steps, they would unfurl and break the windowpane in the back door. I couldn't believe he was placing me in the attic. I could've stayed in the den for the next couple of months until my mother returned. I couldn't believe he would make me give up a bedroom in Baltimore to come here and keep me hidden in the attic. I was sure the decision was not his alone. I had a strong feeling that Della had a great deal of input about where I would sleep. Much to her dismay, I was intruding on her *Better Homes and Gardens* lifestyle. There was no room for me here at this inn.

I was both physically and emotionally drained after I rummaged through the packed suitcases for my robe. I decided that I would put my clothing and belongings away after I arrived from school the next day. My father ascended the rickety stairs with me behind him. I had to duck to maneuver my way in and around what appeared to be nothing more than a storage space with a bed in the back. I followed him to the rear of the attic, where a single twin bed was placed. Next to the bed was a small window which allowed me some relief from the Indian summer. He didn't say much as he wished me a good night. He carefully walked through the maze of clothes and storage boxes and backed his way down the stairs. He turned the light off and I heard him fold the stairs. I watched as the light from the main house disappeared with the closing of the door.

I was so worn out by the events of the day that I didn't bother to pull the covers on me when I turned in. The mattress was worn from Della's son's body and I could feel the springs poke my body as I attempted to make myself comfortable. I looked out the little window to see that my view of anything remotely beautiful was blocked by the house next door. I closed my eyes to prevent myself from crying to sleep, but that was hard to do.

I was awakened by the sounds of the stairs being lowered for my release from hell. I was allowed to get dressed in the den since that is where I hung my clothes for school. My father was up and about getting ready for work. I greeted both him and Della with "good morning." He continued to go about the task of getting ready. She barely opened her mouth. I felt like an outsider. I wanted to run back to Baltimore, but those thoughts were interrupted by Della's granddaughter walking in.

I knew Deborah from the visits I'd had with my father. She was the eldest daughter of my oldest stepsister. We got along pretty well because we were the same age. She lived a few blocks down the street and one block over. Although she never told me, I was convinced that my father had to seriously convince her to take me under her wing for the first few days of school. Deborah was less than a month older than me and she called me "uncle." She was able to accomplish over the summer that one thing I had planned; she had received her driver's license. Her reward for taking me under her wing came with the keys Della handed her to the car my father had purchased Della.

I looked around my new neighborhood on our way to school. Deborah made small talk, but my mind was 150 miles away thinking about my mother. I wondered if she had had a restless sleep as I had. I wondered if she had gone to work or if she had stayed home to cry more. I wish I could have.

We arrived at my new high school. It appeared to me like a haunted mansion in some very bad horror movie. I really hadn't paid much attention to Deborah, her singing and talking about the school. I only exited the car and followed her to the main office. She left me there, but before heading to class, reminded me to meet her at the car at the end of the school day. I sat there waiting for someone to tell me what to do. From the first look of the school upon entering, it was not as modern as my former high school. The interior walls were dark, creating a dismal feel for anyone entering. As we made our way toward the office, I noticed the beautiful hues of the students. Unlike my old school, where I was part of the minority, I was now part of the majority.

As I sat there, I fiddled with my book bag and looked around. I saw more black people making their way in and out of the office in authoritative roles than I had seen in the entire faculty at my old school. I looked down at my watch to check the time and when I looked up, the most elegant black woman greeted me.

Brenda Marshall was her name. She asked me to follow her. We made a right turn out of the main office and headed approximately four doors down to the Guidance Department. As she escorted me into her office she invited me to sit down. She had a beautiful smile. She immediately placed me at ease and informed me that she would be my new guidance counselor. We sat there and she allowed me to share with her what had led to my move to Richmond. I was careful not to reveal too much. I stuck with my story of finding out I had to go to a city school after the county discovered my true address. She reviewed my transcripts and we began to select my courses for the year. I hadn't realized at the time how great an education I was receiving in Baltimore County until Ms. Marshall informed me that my classes and grades had placed me in the Honors Program. *Yeah, right*, I thought. But I went with it. The graduation requirements for my new high school were far more lax than the old one. I actually had more class credits than I needed in some cases. *This was going to be a piece of cake*, I thought. I was upset, however, that the one class I wanted was not offered. In Baltimore, I had enrolled in my second-year journalism course, but this school didn't offer it. Although they did have a drama class, I thought a half of loaf is better than none.

As we finished determining my class schedule, Ms. Marshall informed me that she was there if I needed anything. Her warm smile reminded me of my mother and I thought about her again. It was time to go to my first class. Ms. Marshall called for one of the young student assistants to show me to my class. Her name was Tina. She just happened to be in my two honors classes and would be more than happy to show me around.

I thanked my new lady friend and followed Tina out the door. Although we walked side by side, it was difficult to understand what she was saying due to the acoustics of the cavernous halls. She rattled on about the school, the programs, what to do, what not to do, whom to hang with, and whom to avoid. I was taking all of this information in and watching the students frantically make their way through the halls to head to their class. My eyes focused on the new eccentrics passing me. To my left was a young lady who fashioned a dress out of a set of garbage bags. To my right were the few white students, working what I found out later was called punk-rock fashion. Spiked hair adorned their heads like tribal headdresses. Their eye makeup was heavy and the piercings poking from their lips, eyes and ears looked quite painful. As I made my way through this new zoo, I made sure that I made it to my first class on time. I walked in and handed the teacher my transfer form and felt the eyes of everyone focus on me. By the end of the day, as I met Deborah at the car, everyone knew there was a new kid in town.

Outside of making Ms. Marshall's acquaintance, I hated this new school. I hated my new home. I wanted what was old and familiar. I was in the den working on the homework assignments given to me when my father walked in from work. With half-hearted interest, he asked about my day. I told him that I hated it and I never wanted to go back. I tried to express to him how I felt about the students looking down at me and making comments behind my back. My comments didn't faze him one way or the other. As he got up to go change his work clothes, he told me straight out, "You really don't have a choice." No truer words were spoken after that. I had made my bed and now I had to lie in it. Everything that I loved and cared for was gone. I had to start over and deal with it. I was "cured" of my thoughts of being with boys after the two-week stay in the hospital. These desires had to be suppressed because I couldn't imagine being forced into another hospital stay. It was bad enough that my father felt he was forced to step in and raise me. If I were to start to feel those feelings again, where would I go, what would I do?

I decided to work with the hand I was dealt. I started out well and with good intentions. The class load was easy to deal with because it was actually repeating some of the things I had done in my sophomore year. I didn't have many friends in school outside of Deborah and Tina. My days consisted of going to school, doing homework and watching television. On the occasional Friday, when Della and my father wanted to get me out of the house, they would ante up the money for Deborah and me to go to the high school football games. I would have preferred staying home watching a movie on television or doing additional homework, but the two of them wanted me out of the house. So, Deborah benefited more than I did; she didn't have to pay and all she had to do was get me to the game, place me on one of the bleacher seats and go off with her friends. I would sit there and watch the cheerleaders, looking around at the scoreboard to see how much longer I had to stay. Sometimes if there were no games, there was always a dance. When Deborah got tired of me tagging along, my father knew when and where activities were at my high school and would take me. I went along with this routine day in and day out. As my father reminded me constantly, I had no choice.

Since I was not allowed a television in my attic prison, or a desk for that matter, I was allowed to view television and complete homework in the den. I would sometimes look up from the geometry textbook to catch a commercial or television show to break the monotony of the evening. Della never really had much conversation for me and when my father was home, he was distracted doing other things. One evening while double-checking my homework assignment before I adjourned to the attic, a commercial captured my attention and held it.

A woman, or what appeared to be a woman, was on stage in garish makeup. Her hands were outstretched to the audience and they were enjoying her performance. Further into the commercial spot, I saw the faces of people dancing and having a good time. It reminded me of the night I celebrated my sixteenth birthday. I closed my textbook and glued my eyes to the remainder of the commercial. I flipped to an empty page in my notebook to jot down the name of this place being advertised: Secrets.

I did a little research over the next few weeks without revealing why I needed the information about this place called Secrets. I found through Columbo-like investigation, that Secrets was a gay bar in the lower downtown area of Richmond. At the close of the commercial that had repeated a number of times since I'd first seen it, it provided a street address for all prospective patrons. Up until this point, I had no intention of resurrecting the feelings that landed me here in my father's hours, but I was miserable. I wanted to be around likeminded individuals. I planned ahead of time for that moment. For the first time, to my father's surprise and Della's delight, I asked for permission to attend the high school dance before the two could even mention that there was one coming up.

When we arrived in front of the high school that Friday night, I exited the car, reminding my father that the dance didn't end until midnight. I told him I would catch a ride with one of the numerous girls from school who had discovered my home phone number and were calling on a regular basis. I knew why they were calling, but I didn't have the faintest interest in any of them. But my father happily passed the phone to me when he heard a female's voice on the line.

I headed to the cafeteria where the dance was held and took my place alongside the wall, killing time until the dance was over. I had planned earlier that week to visit this place called Secrets, but I didn't want to arrive too early. I stayed at the dance and endured another evening of folks standing around posing, girls giving attitude and guys attempting to outdance each other. They announced that it was the last dance and I made my way from the crowded cafeteria to the bus stop.

I walked the two or three blocks to Broad Street, the main thoroughfare that ran the length of Richmond. I waited impatiently for the first bus that would take me to downtown and from there, I would make my way to Shockoe Bottom. I was doing it again, but I needed to. I wanted to be me. I couldn't hide the truth I had now come to know. I was gay.

As the bus lurched to a stop in front of the old movie theaters on Broad Street and the closed McDonald's, I noticed how downtown Richmond hadn't really changed since I'd grown up there. The neon sign of Cavalier men's shop was dark but loomed in the downtown darkness. I continued on the bus, as it made its way past the Medical College of Virginia heading toward my final destination.

I exited the bus and made my way to the address I'd jotted down on the piece of paper. The area looked very similar to the old factories that had been abandoned in movies I'd viewed on television. The tobacco factories that became a major staple in the state's economy were now vacant and housed in other parts of the city. As I edged closer to Secrets, it occurred to me the places I attended in Baltimore, similar to the place I was headed, were all off the beaten path. I didn't understand why. I started to see more cars head in the direction I was going. Some of the drivers looked in my direction as they stopped to size me up, but I remained focus and nervous at the same time. My pulse raced knowing that up the street and around the corner was heaven.

I finally arrived. I wiped the beaded perspiration from my brow. The building was enormous compared to the two nightspots I attended in Baltimore. As a matter of fact, I believed that you could sit both of those places in this building and still have room for two other bars. The building alone took up the entire block and it was well lit, unlike the place where I'd had my first dance with Michael. I walked in, heading toward the counter, with my money already in hand to gain entrance.

"ID, please," oozed out of the mouth of the fresh-faced male working the counter. *Oh shit, I don't have ID*, I thought. I didn't need it before. I assumed there was a brotherhood to going to a gay club, but I realized friendship was the one thing that allowed me in the spot where Alex worked. I hoped by telling him I was new to town it would allow me entrance. "I'm sorry, I can't let you in without ID," was his response. There was a line forming behind me. "Next."

I stepped out of the way to decide what to do next. I stood there realizing there was nothing I could do. I headed back toward the main door to find a cab and head home. As I walked the hall of shame and embarrassment, the guy who placed the band of entry on your arm followed me. He apologized and informed me it was the law not to allow anyone under twenty-one into the establishment, nothing personal. I knew that I couldn't pass for twenty-one. He read the defeated look on my face and informed me, that after two o'clock, they stopped serving alcohol. At that time; I would be able to enter. He suggested that I come back another night. I smiled a polite *thank you* in his direction as he made his way back to the counter. I stood there at the door trying to figure how to get out of this dilemma. Each time I saw a cab pass by, there was some drunken passenger already occupying it. When I was in Baltimore I didn't have to deal with this; Carol was there, but now it was a whole new ballgame.

As I stood there contemplating my next move, I saw a black guy walk in. He stopped and smiled. He asked if I was going in and I told him the bad news that I had been refused entry because of my age. He apologized. I asked if he had a moment to talk and he informed me he was meeting a friend. I said, "Okay," and he walked a few feet away. He turned back and told me to wait, he would return. I stayed in place waiting for him. I was excited to see he was a man of his word, I was happy to see that he returned. Not because he was an attractive man, I will give him that, but the reason was something totally different. During the times I'd hung out with Carol, Alex and Michael in Baltimore, I never saw anyone remotely similar to me. I never saw anyone black.

When he returned, he introduced himself. I told him my story in a nut-shell. I had just moved to Richmond from Baltimore and I had seen the commercial for Secrets. He laughed. "It gets them every time." He continued to let me know that he didn't have a lot of time, but wanted to come back as promised. Within a few minutes of his initial disappearance, he had written down his phone number and suggested that I give him a call. At the moment he handed me his number, his buddy walked up to see what was taking him so long. That would be the first black man to sweep me off my feet. Literally. His name was David.

Have you ever watched the old westerns featuring John Wayne? Well, imagine his swagger on the frame of a six-foot-four beautiful black man. His hair was cut close, giving the appearance from a distance that he was bald. He made his way toward my new friend and me. He opened his mouth, allowing me the pleasure of hearing his deep Barry White voice. "What's up?" We were introduced by my new friend and as I reached to shake his hand, my tiny fingers disappeared in his massive claw. *Damn!*

My new friend wanted to go back inside the club to have a good time. I promised him that I would call as he walked away with his buddy. David inspected me again with his eyes before he nodded in my direction and followed my new friend. I wanted so much to join them, but I knew the rules now. I watched as this beautiful black man walked away, smiling once again before he turned the corner and disappeared. I knew I would see him again, but when? The invitation was extended by our mutual friend to call. I stored the number in my wallet as I hailed the next cab and knew that he would be hearing from me soon, real soon.

chapter eight

The cab door broke the silence in the stillness of the middle-class neighborhood I called home. Unlike the endless rows of apartments on Lodestone Way, the Georgia Avenue stretch showcased manicured lawns and carefully pruned bushes. Della spent a great deal of her free time from her part-time job, on her knees masterfully replicating the images from magazines to frame the rancher. The bright streetlights warned intruders that the homeowners were watching and wanted to keep this piece of the West End intact. I walked the length of the bricked walkway to enter my father's house. It wasn't too late this time, so I would probably get a light talking to. I turned the knob on the screen door only to see that it had been locked. On another failed attempt to open it, my father opened the solid mahogany door to see me standing there.

He unlocked the screen door to allow me to enter. I could tell he was a little upset. He moved a little out of the way to allow me to make my way to the kitchen, where the entrance to the attic was located. I thought I had gotten away with it, but he stopped me as I placed the stool where he instructed me to lower the ladder. "Why are you coming in here late, boy?" I hadn't prepared a lie this time. There was no usual discussion of going to Harborplace to cover my tracks and I hadn't been in Richmond long enough to find an equivalent place of gathering. I told him my newfound high school friends and I had gone out after the dance to eat and I lost track of time. I wasn't going to crack. He thought of my response and from his response, it worked. As I had done so many times, I allowed my hands to guide me up the stairs to the attic, hearing him as I pulled the ladder to close the door within the ceiling. "Don't start this now." But, this was only the beginning.

My first black gay male friend Roy, whom I met my first night at Secrets, educated me about the city. During these lessons, he told me about the city, the hot spots and in some ways, provided me the education I needed to get to and from wherever I needed. It was nice to have someone who was familiar with what I was going through. I reluctantly gave him my number, knowing that he would be the first guy to call the house, but I could cover my tracks with my father on that one. But it was his friend, the black John Wayne, who gave my father reason to question, "Who is this man calling the house?"

Roy had mentioned to me his friend David also wanted my number to call and I granted him permission to share it with him. Within minutes of my okaying the request, I was on the phone with David.

I found out in our conversation that David was from New York and attending Virginia State University. His voice dripped sweet nothings in my ear as we talked. I didn't realize at the time, the city in which Virginia State was located was considered a long distance call. He stayed off campus at a local house where other VSU students resided. He was able to call me daily before my father arrived home from work because he, like many other college students at that time, had been given an illegal long distance code. They would run the code up and the billing, until the telephone company figured out what was going on. I made sure that I was always near the phone, so that no one would answer it but me. On the occasion that I was performing chores and Della or my father answered, I was given a few minutes to chat. I had no privacy in this place. The quarters were small and everything I said was being monitored, or so I felt. I had to talk in codes, especially when my father was around.

"Who is the grown-ass man calling you?" he would ask as I hung up the receiver. By this time, I had lying down to a science. "It was so-and-so's brother," I'd respond as I exited the den to continue my chores.

When the long distance telephone scam caught up with David and the other students in the boardinghouse, I would call him. My father noticed when he received the monthly phone bill; there were pages upon pages of long distance calls to the Petersburg area. I played dumb, stating that I didn't know VSU was a long distance extension. I knew it was, but David couldn't call me.

When we were able to spend time together it was spent in his room off campus carrying on. He towered over me when he stood before me and covered me completely when we were lying down. Our intimacy was limited to kissing and the occasional blowjob. We mutually agreed that for the moment that's all we would engage in. My few experiences with guys, namely Michael and Ken, found me inside of them, not the other way around. That was a bridge I didn't want to cross. I couldn't imagine the thought of someone putting their dick in me and me receiving pleasure from it. David was like me in a sense. He wouldn't let me fuck him either and after a while, we both walked away embracing a friendship, never carrying it any further than that.

I would see David on occasion while I was out with Roy and we were pleasant with each other; there was no reason not to be. We started as friends and we ended as such. Roy became my guardian angel. He was able to pick me up from school dances to transport me to Secrets when we agreed to go out. During my friendship with him, he even introduced me to his other friends. I was really beginning to like this gay thing.

The relationship at home with my father was a different story. Each weekend after homework was completed, chores done, I found myself hanging out. He and Della stopped encouraging me to go to school functions. I would arrive home later and later during the morning hours. My father would sit there in the dark, allowing me to creep only so far before he flipped the light switch, telling me yet again, "What did I tell you about coming in this late?"

I would respond as if replaying the same cued-up tape, "I'm sorry, I won't do it again." But I continued to be defiant.

One night while standing at the end of the enclosed dance floor of Secrets, I looked around to see dancers with outstretched hands who were screaming at the top of their lungs to Fonda Rae's "Touch Me." Out of the corner of my eye, I saw the man who shouted louder than any other.

He was in his own world. His eyes were closed, in deep thought as his muscular body made inviting gestures to all who watched him. He wore a white sweat suit with the logo "N2U" perfectly centered across his chest. I was still in my preppy stage of dress, sporting a pair of burgundy dress slacks, with pale-pink pin-stripes, a pink oxford and a rose-colored sweater. Now that I look back, pink was the suitable color for this place. I was so mesmerized by this man's ability to tune out all things and enjoy himself. He would play both roles in a tango, switching sides in this dance to serve as his own partner. I inched closer and closer to him. When he decided to stop for a moment and wipe the sweat drenching his body, I decided to step closer. He raised the bottle of water to his mouth, allowing me to view the massive arms that came from working out, or so I thought.

As he caught his breath and I found mine, I inched closer once more until I was in his space. I parted my trembling lips and asked him to dance. His face searched mine as he gave me the once-over, similar to that look David had given me when we'd first met. "No." Another song came on and he was back to his one-man dance.

My heart raced as I headed to the bathroom. I looked in the mirror at the frightened face looking back at me. I had heard of straight guys going to gay bars because they liked the music and they also knew straight women would be there with their gay male friends. I had asked a straight guy to dance and he was going to whip my ass when I left. I hid out in the men's room, and every now and then I would look back at the dance floor to see if he was still there. When I noticed that he was gone, I quickly left and vowed the next time I wanted to dance, I would follow his lead and serve as my own dance partner.

ഗ്രൈ

Things were getting increasingly worse at home. The few months my mother said I would be staying with my father had been extended indefinitely, as she underwent a series of tests in Baltimore to determine whether she had multiple sclerosis. My hate for this place was continuing to grow. Della continued her dislike for me and she showed me every chance she could, out of view of my father. He rarely had enough time for me as well. I found my comfort in disobeying him and staying out until the wee hours. Whatever threats my father made about cutting off my allowance or punishing me became jokes. How could he possibly think, after sixteen years, that he could or would tell me what to do? When he had the opportunity to teach me right from wrong, he decided to leave this in the hands of my mother. It was not his cross to bear. I would sit and allow my sad look to convince him I knew I was wrong for what I'd done. Then I'd turn around the next minute and defy his authority. When I'd wanted a relationship with him, he didn't give it. Now that he wanted my respect, I didn't give it.

₭⇒℁

It was cold the evening Roy and I visited Secrets. We were warmed by the heat of the bodies dancing around us. I never consumed alcohol on the premises because I knew that I would be immediately removed and never allowed in until I turned twenty-one. That was the only rule I lived by in a city that had brought me new rules in my life. As the houselights slowly rose to alert the patrons to get the fuck out and go home, Roy and I made our way to the side door. Roy's friend was riding with us and wanted to take a moment and say good night to some friends. As Roy and I waited, I noticed his friend embracing the John Travolta impersonator from only a few weeks earlier. We were within earshot of their conversation and I heard him ask, "Who's that?" Now Mr. "N2U" was "N2Me."

I excused myself from Roy's conversation and walked over to him. Roy had taught me how to talk the talk and so I did. "Hi." I extended my hand as he received it in his. "I asked you to dance a couple of weeks ago and you denied me the pleasure." I looked in his eyes. "If you would like to know anything about me, ask me." I pivoted on the balls of my feet, said good night and headed out the door. I smiled at my boldness as Allen—his name I found out—was stunned.

He took my suggestion. He asked me about me when he called my house. I found out that a phone number can easily be given up by friends, if the right persuasive tactics are used—the promise of a drink, a rolled joint or a fellow phone number in exchange. However he got the number, I was happy to hear his voice. I gave him directions to pick me up to give me the official tour of Richmond. It was a beautiful Sunday afternoon. Although the weather had turned cool, it was nice enough to remove the T-tops in the Camaro he had borrowed from a friend. I discovered him and he had discovered me.

He stood maybe an inch shorter than me at about five feet ten inches. He was a medium-brown complexion with a body to boot. That had been clearly displayed the first night I saw his python-like arms. His height carried the defined muscles he showed off very well when he removed his shirt while dancing alone. His smile invited you into his world, on his terms, but he made sure you were welcomed. He would lean in his car, close enough to me, so that if he felt the desire to turn his head toward me, our lips would not have far to travel for a stolen kiss before the traffic light turned green, giving us permission to proceed. His taste in music was definitely a little different than mine. I was used to the head-banging heavy metal of Def Leppard and he introduced me to the bass-driven sounds of house music. We were polar opposites. With barely a trace of facial hair and skin so pale, without sunlight I looked almost emaciated. But we clicked.

We spent hours on the phone conversing when we were apart, laughing at stupid shit. I would slouch down on the sofa in the den, knowing better than to have Della walk back and catching me lying down. I would notice her looking in at me from the kitchen, wondering who placed this laughter in my heart that she tried so hard to silence.

To get me out of the house and allow me to spend more time with him, Allen got me my first job in high school. I worked as a cashier alongside his assistant managerial position at a local fast-food restaurant. When I informed my father that I had a part-time job and Allen was instrumental in getting it for me, he immediately took a liking to him. I didn't have to lie about our friendship. I did, however, lie about how we met. But I was saved from further lying when I discovered Tina, my tour guide and classmate from my first day of school, was Allen's cousin. She made it her goal to tell me, after seeing Allen pick me up from school one afternoon. During work hours, we pretended we were cousins for the sake of the staff. Although he got me the job, I proved myself worthy of their respect by taking shifts to accommodate single mothers who needed to take time off for their kids. Everything was going well for me. I still missed my mother, but I found a substitution for her absence in the time I spent with Allen.

We continued getting to know each other. At twenty, he still lived at home and so did I. I couldn't freely invite him over to hang out, because of the limited space in my father's house. Nor could I visit him because of his large family. The quiet times we spent together were reserved for the back-seat of his sister's car in a secluded area where he grew up. Much like my physical involvement with David, our intimacy was still limited to blowjobs and kissing. Sometimes at his urging, I would allow him to place his dick between my legs, to feel some other warmth outside of my mouth, but that was it. We never crossed the line to anal penetration. I was not ready for something like that and the pain I assumed it would bring.

Every time I found happiness in my short life up until that point, some-thing would inevitably swoop down and take it away from me. Things were going well with school, I had a job, and I had a boyfriend. My father was still riding my ass about me staying out late on weekends, but I managed to get around this on occasion by saying I was working late and helping out with inventory.

One Sunday, Allen picked me up from work. It was raining that day and I still didn't have a car. He didn't have to work this particular Sunday shift. My father was happy that Allen was in my life. He didn't know to what extent our friendship had developed, but it took the burden off him of being a father. Allen was A-okay in his book. And he was A-okay in mine.

Before he dropped me off at home that Sunday, Allen and I walked around the fountain park located a few streets from my house. I could tell something was bothering him, but I didn't know how to ask. I shared the rundown of my day at work, waiting for him to interject and tell me what was on his mind. The rain started to pick up its pace, as we rushed to seek shelter in his sister's car. We sat there for a moment before he started the engine to allow the heat to blast and warm us.

I couldn't wait any longer for him to tell me what was on his mind. I wanted to know what this silence was between us. We sat there, listening to the engine humming and he told me. My mouth dropped when I heard his dilemma.

"I don't think I can see you anymore." With that, I turned to stare out the window.

"Why?" I asked, wanting to know what could possibly make him feel this way. He told me that he had needs and although he was falling in love with me, he wanted to take the relationship further. He knew I didn't want to try getting fucked at the time and decided to go seek it somewhere else. I continued to stare out the window, stunned. When he reached for me to look at him, I turned away. Since his attempt to get me to face him failed, he reached over and handed me an envelope. I snatched it from his hands and let it rest in my lap for a few minutes. If he didn't want to see me anymore, why would he give me a card?

I opened the card and saw the pastel colors swirling on the cover, giving the illusion of a beautiful sunrise, unlike this dark cloud hovering over us now. I opened the card and read the notation, "Everywhere I go, my thoughts of you go with me." I read it over and over again, even his signature, "Love Allen." I wanted so much for Allen to remain in my life that I would do anything to keep him there. As much as I tried to please my father with everything I did, I could never get him to reciprocate the feelings of love I had for him. If I allowed Allen inside of me, could I show him how much I cared for him? Would he stay with me? Would he love me the way I had wanted and searched for in Michael's bed? Could he give me what I wanted so much from my father? His love.

I decided at that moment to give in to his desires. I wanted so much to hold on to him that I decided to endure a few brief moments of pain. When I consented to his wishes, we made our way to the secluded spot close to his home. En route, we stopped by the local 7-Eleven convenience store for a few essentials. I nervously sat in the car until he returned with his bag of supplies. He wouldn't allow me to look into the bag. He placed it in the backseat and we headed toward the road leading to the dirt path of our hideaway.

Allen had parked and made his way to the backseat. I listened to the radio for a few more minutes before I joined him. I removed the ten-dollar vintage coat I had purchased at the Goodwill and folded it neatly. I reached and handed it to him to create the effect of a pillow for my head. I didn't want to open the car door to turn on the lights, alerting passing cars to where we were located. I followed Allen's lead and crawled through the seat opening to join him. We sat there for a moment. This was new to me, being on the receiving end, but I knew that I needed to do this in order to keep him.

He grabbed my face to kiss me. I loved kissing him and I could tell the feeling was mutual, even if I smelled like the chicken sold at the fast-food restaurant. We parted for a moment and he whispered, "We don't have to do this, if you don't want to." But I did. I loved him and I wanted to show him. I assisted him in unzipping his jeans and removing his shoes. He slid the jeans off and just reared back in his briefs. He helped me remove the chicken-scented smock and the rest of my clothing. There was a chill in the air so we unfolded the coat to create a blanket for us. He grabbed the back of my head and guided me to his crotch as he had many times. I enjoyed the combination of sweetness and musk in my mouth as I sucked his dick. His head was resting on the top of the backseat, as I continued to swallow him in my mouth. I made sure to leave some residue of saliva on the head to use as lubricant. He was not a small guy, although the package that contained him would lead you to believe otherwise. He fumbled for the bag that he had placed in the backseat from 7-Eleven and pulled out a small jar. Then he reached into his jeans that now rested on the floor of the backseat and retrieved a small bottle, similar to the one that Michael had first introduced me to.

I removed the bottle from his hand so that I could have control over it. In the meantime, he opened the jar. I could only make out that the little container was red. When Allen reached in to remove its contents, I noticed that it was blue. Before I exited the car that evening, I needed to ease my curiosity and find out what it was. He applied the blue substance to his rock-hard dick. He then reached for a little more to apply to my virgin opening. What was left on his hand was rubbed into his hairy chest that I envied. He sat waiting for me.

I unscrewed the top of the bottle of poppers and inhaled the contents as I had done the summer night I met Michael. With Allen sitting there, I crawled over him, straddling him while I faced him. I took his dick and guided it slowly into me. I winced in pain as I felt the head of him attempt to enter me. I still had control of the little bottle and inhaled once again. There was that old familiar rush of warmth filling my body. This time, because of my love for Allen, I held my breath and let him in.

I cried, as he slowly rocked my waist back and forth until he was completely in. I could feel the remains of this sticky blue substance now on my face as he forced me to look at him. He wiped my tears and kissed me. He allowed me to wait a moment as I became used to this foreign invader. He leaned forward, forcing my back against the front seat of the driver's side allowing him further entry into me.

We stayed in this position for a few moments. I continued to cry and I wanted to scream, but he was happy. He placed his strong hands around the small of my back and laid me on the backseat of the car. He raised my legs higher so that he could have access to the spot he wanted. My feet were planted firmly on the roof of the car and I could no longer kiss him in this position. I was distracted by the pain. Although the moment didn't last very long, if felt like hours had passed. When it was over, Allen removed himself from me and rested his head on my chest. I eventually stopped crying.

We made another stop at 7-Eleven before he took me home. This time, he didn't need a bag for his purchases. He returned with a pre-wrapped long-stemmed rose and handed it to me. While he was in the store searching for it, I reached behind the driver's seat to see what were the bluish contents of the red container. I removed it from the bag and read the label: Bergamot hair dressing.

When I finally arrived home, my stomach was aching and my body was sore—not only from the experience of being fucked for the first time, but from the various positions I'd twisted and turned my body to accommodate him. I apologized to my father for being late after informing him Allen and I were hanging out after work. I still smelled of the chicken grease, even though I worked the front register. I excused myself as I took a shower to remove the smell of poultry and to soothe the throbbing behind me. As I leaned my backside toward the showerhead for the hot water to hit it, I saw traces of blood run down my left leg and into the drain. I smiled a little through the pain, hoping as he made his way home, he was smiling as well. That was March 31, 1985. Some things you will never forget.

సించ

My happiness up to this point was based on a lie. Everything was well with school, Allen and I continued to grow, and I finally realized what love was. Unfortunately, it was a love I needed to keep confident between Allen and me and the few friends I had made since moving to Richmond. My mother's return had been delayed indefinitely as I saw the end of my junior year approaching. I wanted so much to share with her these new feelings I had, or rather the feelings I had suppressed all this time, but she was not around. I knew that I couldn't tell my father. Our conversations were still limited to "hi," "bye" and "see ya later." My mother had always been my strongest supporter and I couldn't lie any longer. It was time to open the rest of my world to her.

Outside of the gay characters that appeared for comic relief in television and movies, there was one gay character that I actually identified with—Steven Carrington. I faithfully watched the ABC show *Dynasty* to see how he dealt with his sexuality. During one episode, Steven introduced his father, Blake, to his boyfriend. Seeing this display of his braveness, I picked up the phone and called my mother long distance. It was time for me to be brave.

It was always good to hear her voice. She was preparing for bed when I reached her. As always, we started out our conversations with what was going on in our separate worlds. She knew the relationship with Della was not a good one, but continued to encourage me to hang in there. After the exchanges of pleasantries, she would always ask if something was wrong. In the past, I would say "no." I didn't want to alert her ahead of time of my revelation, so I would tell her how well I was doing in school and how much I enjoyed my job.

When I hesitated to tell her things she was used to hearing, she asked again. I whispered softly into the receiver so that my father or Della wouldn't hear me, "Mom, I think I am bisexual." The way this played out in my mind, I expected her to say, "Good for you," but she didn't. I heard the tears fall the same way they did when we said good-bye several months earlier.

"I knew it, I knew it. What did I do wrong?" she asked. I couldn't think of anything she'd done to have made me this way. I tried to comfort her and tell her it wasn't her fault. I wanted to reach through the phone to hug her, to take away her pain, but I couldn't. I also couldn't continue to lie to myself and hide the feelings that I was having. It would have been so much easier to live my life the way she had planned for me; get married, have kids, but I knew that it wasn't in the cards. If I had done that, I would have been miserable, only to make someone else happy.

She stopped crying for a moment. She didn't offer any words or support or consolation. She said that she was disappointed and that I'd better tell my father. She was going to speak with him the very next day to see if I had done as she instructed. Way to go. That was the last thing I needed at this point. My mother and I had always had special little secrets between the two of us and I wanted this to remain one of them. If she handled this information like she did, how was he going to deal with it?

I walked out of the den after hanging up the phone. This was the first time that my father and I would ever have a heart-to-heart conversation and I wasn't sure how to approach him. I knocked on his bedroom door and asked if he could join me in the den; I needed to talk with him.

I turned the television off, after watching Steven's courage and hoped that it would somehow float my way. I fidgeted with my hands, hoping that the answers would come to me. I found a spot on the floor to stare at as I opened my mouth. I repeated to him what I'd told my mother.

There was a disturbing silence after I revealed my secret. I looked up slowly, staring at him to see if I could read his reaction. We sat there for approximately twenty minutes with dead silence. I attempted to delve into his thoughts, but the answers didn't come easily. Without looking at me, my father stood up and walked out of the den. As he headed toward his bedroom, he instructed me to go to bed. I figured it would be in my best interest now to follow his rules for once. I removed myself from the sofa and headed to the attic.

෨෬

Over the next couple of days things were the same as they had been since I'd arrived here. Very little conversation had been shared or exchanged between the three of us and it was as if I had said nothing to him. If there was something bothering him, he never showed any sign. He was never one who spoke to me a lot in the afternoons anyway, so I just assumed that it was okay. That is until we went to dinner.

Della had decided that she was not cooking that Friday evening. My father and I had to fend for ourselves if we wanted nourishment. My father told me to get in the car and we headed out for a quick bite to eat.

This was not one of the dinners where we would sit down and try to find small talk. He wanted something quick and he got it. After we left the drive-thru of the fast-food restaurant, my father abruptly stopped the car and placed it in reverse. The bag in my lap slid a little as I caught the contents before they landed on the floor.

"You mean to tell me you would rather spend your time with a bunch of fags, than a group of young ladies like that?" He pointed his finger toward a group of young ladies waiting for the local bus.

Why did he have to wait until now? Had he done this after I told him two nights ago, I would have been better prepared. "Dad, I told you I was bisexual, not gay," was the only response I could counter with. I thought that would be easier to digest rather than come out completely.

He placed the car in "drive" and continued, "It's all the same to me."

After my father's outburst, everything I did reminded him of being gay. Whether it was something I wore, or if I spent too much time on the telephone, I was being gay. It became unbearable. The only solace I had was leaving school and going directly to work at my part-time job. Even then, I had to make sure that I was home when he said to be there; being late meant I was out being gay.

At this time, he started to ask more questions about Allen. He wanted to know if Allen was the "one" who had made me this way. He put his foot down with new rules. He didn't want Allen calling the house anymore. He didn't want Allen picking me up from work. The guy that he raved about so much before now became a bitter enemy. He even went as far as to say if Allen wanted to see me, he would have to come to the door and ask my father's permission. If I didn't feel gay at that point, I certainly did when Allen knocked on the door one evening to ask my father if he could speak with me.

I somehow managed to keep a safe distance between my father and Allen. By this time, my father had exposed my deep, dark, dirty little secret to Della. She would walk past me and turn her noise up at me. I knew that our time would come. I had been preparing for it. So when it happened, I was prepared.

It was close to the end of the school year. I started to repeat the behavior of cutting class as I did prior to leaving Baltimore so that I could spend more time with Allen without my father's knowledge. On occasion I would speak with my grandmother and express to her my unhappiness. I couldn't call my mother because I didn't want to worry her.

During a conversation with Grandma, she asked me when was the last time I'd spoken with my mother. I told her it had been a couple of weeks. She told me to call her as soon as I hung up the telephone. I did.

I could hear something in my mother's voice. She really couldn't talk because she was at work. She asked me what I was doing. I thought she meant at that moment, but she didn't. Della had called my mother and informed her that I was trying to ruin her marriage. "He's staying out all hours of the night, thinking he can do whatever the hell he wants," she'd told my mother. "If you don't come and get him soon, we are going to have to put him out." End of discussion.

I was pissed. Not so much at the threat of being removed from the house—hell, I didn't want to be there in the first place—but because Della had called my mother. She knew that my mother was having health issues but she was such a cold-hearted bitch, that she didn't care. When she walked in from her pottery class, I asked to speak with her.

I had to eat humble pie for a bit; it was still uncertain when my mother would be returning and I needed a place to lay my head. I knew that my actions had painted me in a corner and I needed to find a way to rectify it.

I was angry and upset, but softened my approach toward Della. I knew that she was the one who wore the pants in the relationship with my father. I asked nicely if we could attempt to get along for the remainder of my stay and also for my father's sake. She didn't answer. I knew that she was enjoying the fact that I was groveling at this point. She was not receptive at all to my pleas. As I continued to talk with her, or rather *at* her, I decided nicely to tell her that I didn't appreciate her calling my mother, considering the health issues my mother had at the time. What she said next showed me what kind of a bitch she truly was.

"I don't care about you or your mother." I could see joy on her face when she was finally able to reveal this to me. We both knew how she felt, but this was her time to actually show it. By this time, I kissed nice good-bye. Since she shared with me how she felt, I felt obliged to do the same. I didn't care. I told her I hated her and wished my father would beat the living shit out of her. But, I didn't stop there. Since she'd pulled cards about my mother, I had to let this cunt know what her own family thought about her. If she hadn't been a bitch all of her life, maybe she would have had the love and respect of her family, I reminded her. The truth must have sunk in, because she didn't like it. I was able to move away from her and make my way out the door as my father pulled up. I tried explaining to him what had happened, but as always, he didn't listen.

By the time I had gotten off work that evening, their door was closed as I stretched my ears to hear the discussion. I decided to go to bed without showering that night and rest my thoughts. I decided to go to school the next day to avoid contact with Della. I feared that another run-in would result in someone being hurt.

Within twenty-four hours, she was gone. She had packed her things, actually an overnight bag, and left for her mother's house. When I got home from school, my father informed me that she had left him and we needed to start doing for ourselves. *That bitch never did anything for me*, I thought.

I looked over at him and he showed hurt on his face. He looked as if he'd lost his best friend and within a few weeks, he would lose his son.

The school year had come to a close and I barely squeaked by. I was performing in the musical "Don't Bother Me, I Can't Cope" for a summer run at the local outdoor amphitheater. It was ironic that my great solo was a song titled, "My Name is Man," and yet I didn't feel like one. After coming out to my father, he had placed so many restrictions on me, what I could do, when I could do it, and with whom I could do it. If anything, I felt like his daughter more so than his son.

Della returned home on a Friday with a shit-eating grin on her face. My father informed me that he was taking her out of town for the weekend and wanted me to stay with my grandmother. They needed time to sort out some things. I noticed that some of my belongings were in the den so I packed there. All the while, her eyes followed me as if to tell me, she was the better bitch. And she was. During the ride to my grandmother's, I was told in no uncertain terms that I could never return to my father's house. This was his way of cutting the ties that bound us. At some point when the wounds had healed, I would be allowed to return to retrieve the remainder of my belongings.

I can't say that I was hurt. I was pissed more than anything else. Here was a man who had stepped in to fulfill a promise he'd made to my mother, but in less than a year, he'd allowed a woman to interfere. I can't say that I blamed him; I was hell at sixteen years old. I didn't know any better. He was supposed to be the "male role model" in my life, make me a man. But it didn't happen. I was on my own and on stage. Although I felt like an abandoned little boy, I belted out for all attendees to hear, "My Name is Man."

I contacted Allen to let him know what was going on. I don't know why, outside of the fact that he was my boyfriend; he was not in a position to allow me to stay with him since he lived at home as well. Within a week's time, I had three different places of dwelling. I didn't stay more than a few days with Grandma because my aunt and I didn't get along and the only other relative in a position to help me out lived in the projects. I stayed there while she was in the hospital with Allen a few days, playing house with Allen because I had no place to go.

He was my only source of strength at the time. Seeing that I was in dire straits, he decided that it was time for the two of us to move in together. He found a local boardinghouse that had a large room that we shared. For the summer, we lived together and I thought everything was great. I had found the love that my father never gave me in this childlike man. But that happiness would soon be interrupted.

80CB

After Allen made me his houseboy/husband, I started to see the flaws in him. On weekends during my summer before entering my senior year in high school, Allen had begun to leave me on Saturday evenings and not return to me until late Sunday. He journeyed to what I would eventually discover for myself, the black gay mecca of Washington, D.C. There was a club located in the northwest area of Washington, where Allen would go, drop a tab of acid and dance his cares away. He, of course, would spend the night there with friends and I believed him. They were the same friends who called and spoke to me. But upon his return, after he crashed and burned, he would snuggle next to me, holding me tight, making me feel secure, and he would mumble names. The first few times I chalked it up to the music still dancing in his head. But these were audible and clear names of individuals who were not his friends.

I tried my best to pull my weight with Allen. I continued to work and I was getting more hours since school was out, but he continued to leave me on weekends. On the chance that I would have off, I would do laundry and clean thoroughly so that when he returned home or what we called home, it was nice and prepared for him.

When it was time to do laundry, as my mother taught me, I found myself emptying pockets to make sure nothing remained in the clothing. And that's when I started to discover numbers. There weren't numbers of friends that we both knew; no, these were numbers of friends Allen had made while dancing the night away in D.C.

When I confronted him, he always had an excuse. I always believed him. I had no choice. They were his friends in D.C. who had recently moved and had their new numbers ready for him when they saw him at the club. But I wasn't stupid. Some of the same names that he called out in his sleep while holding me, matched the names that appeared on the numerous slips of paper and matchbook covers I found in his pockets.

I couldn't argue with him about it; if I did, he would put me out and I had no place to turn. I didn't want to go back to the projects, so I would lie there while he slept, holding me, wondering who he was thinking of in his dreams.

I figured what was good for the goose was also good for the gander. I started meeting other guys at Secrets when Allen headed to D.C. There was no one significant. By this time, Allen and I decided to remain just friends. We would remain friends with benefits. Between the two of us, we acknowledged in some way that we were still a couple and I continued to say to others I met that I was involved—but he didn't. While hanging out at Secrets, I met someone from D.C. who invited me up. Although I went, it wasn't a bad trip, but my heart was still with Allen.

He informed me a couple of days before his departure, he was heading to the Big Apple. His itinerary consisted of him making a stop in D.C. to hang out for a bit and then on to New York. From there, he would travel back through Washington and return to Richmond. I decided to do the same.

I waited until I assumed he had returned to Washington for his last few nights of fun. I was hurt that he never extended the invitation to me to attend, but we were just friends with benefits.

I found my way around Washington in my burgundy Chevette that I named Alice. My father had purchased another car for me, but upon seeing it, Della decided she would take the new one and handed over to me the used Chevette. I maneuvered the poorly paved streets to the place I'd first attended with the guy I'd visited earlier that summer. It was no bigger than a bread box, but I was among beautiful black men. I really didn't pay much attention to the faces; I was only looking for one in particular, Allen.

The evening ended without me catching one glimpse of him. I felt defeated. I was hoping that I would run in to him and that he would be happy to see I'd made the journey to D.C. to find him. From there, we would spend the rest of the weekend together recapturing the love that was fading. But that never happened. What I did receive that weekend was a swollen jaw, confinement and the biggest fear of my life.

I hopped in my car and circled the hole-in-the-wall a few more times to see if maybe I had missed Allen. Traffic was at a standstill as the bar patrons spilled out of the watering hole to take up show on the sidewalk. As I sat there in my car waiting for permission to pass, a gentleman, or so I thought, approached my car and introduced himself. He seemed to be genuinely nice and even concerned about my welfare. He invited me to his house. I didn't know anyone else in D.C. outside of the guy I had visited, so I decided to go. I wanted to rest for a brief moment before I headed back to Richmond and the emptiness of the boarding room Allen and I shared. It was the worst decision of my life.

We sat on his sofa talking about everything and nothing at all. At least it allowed me to kill some time before I got back on the highway to make the two-hour drive back home. My mission was a failure, so it was time to return. Before I could leave, he started to rub my leg. I asked him nicely and politely not to do that. He inched his way closer to me and I retorted, "If the only reason you invited me over here was to have sex, I'm sorry to disappoint you, but I am not interested." I thanked him for his hospitality and got up to make my exit. That's when it happened.

This kind gentleman, who had showed concern, became my captor. His shadow and presence towered me. He possessed not only height, but weight. As my hand reached for the doorknob to let myself out, from behind, I felt the impact of his fist against the side of my face. My hand that reached for the doorknob was now holding the spot of impact, as the hot tears streamed down my cheek. "You're not going anywhere," came out of his mouth as he grabbed me and pushed me onto the sofa. The view from the sofa allowed me to see that he had numerous locks on his door. From the assumption running through my head, this was not a safe neighborhood. He demanded my car keys. Fearing his blow again, I did. In one of the locks, he removed the key to the deadbolt and walked away. He made his way over to me and stroked my face. I begged him not to hit me again. He didn't, but after what happened next, I would have rather endured the beating.

He grabbed me and forced me in front of him. He directed me to his bedroom and told me to remove my clothes. His breath was hot from the alcohol he had consumed, making me want to vomit as he forced his way into my mouth. I stood there trembling as he removed his clothes. I tried not to let him see me cry but I couldn't see his face from the tears welling up in my eyes. I attempted to hide my exposed body with one hand, while rubbing the soreness in my face with the other. He pushed me onto the bed with force and then he raped me.

I bit my lip from the pain. The flashbacks of Allen making love to me were not like this. The memories of Allen's touch and gentleness showed me how tender and loving someone could be when you give them the gift of your body. This man forced himself into me without consideration. He grunted as he held me down, forcing himself deeper in me. I dared not scream because I feared being hit again. The few moments it took him to finish, I tried to focus on living and not the pain. My body was sore from him resting on me and the savage attack I had just undergone. He held me so I wouldn't move. I asked for permission to go to the bathroom, hoping that I could have a minute to gather my thoughts and plan what to do next. I knew that guys could catch sexually transmitted diseases and there was a new one out. I was hoping I could wash up and decrease the chances of catching anything. I rested my hands on the basin, crying silently. I ran the water in the sink, disguising the sobs. I heard him call for me because he thought I was taking too much time in the bathroom. I wiped my eyes and returned. He told me he loved me. He told me he wanted me to stay with him no matter what happened. He showed me pictures of him doing to others what he had just done to me. This aroused him once again and once again he raped me.

He didn't go to sleep until the sun began to rise. I lay there pretending that I was asleep, so that he would not hurt me again. I felt weak and bruised from this man's violation and I wanted to die. Once he figured that I was asleep, he left.

I waited to hear the door close. At the same time I heard the door, I heard the clicks of the locks, locking me in this hell. My knees could barely hold me as I walked around the bedroom looking for my clothes. I found them and got dressed. No matter what I thought, I was going to get out of there. But he had my car keys. I looked for a window that would be my escape. Unfortunately, because the apartment was on the ground level, there were bars preventing anyone entry or exit. I peered out the window hoping for a sign. I happened to see a couple walking and I called out to them. I asked them to call the police. I guess they didn't hear me through the sobs, but I begged them to do so. They continued to walk away and my pleas fell silent.

I sat there as I heard the door. I hoped that he had not heard me calling out for help and apparently he didn't. He smiled at me as if nothing had happened; he came over to me and kissed me. I could still taste the alcohol.

At that moment, when I thought I would have to endure his attack again, there was a knock at the door. He whispered to me, "Don't say a fucking word." It was the police. The couple had heard me.

He peered through the peephole, but didn't answer the door. There was another knock. Since they didn't receive any response, they left. I wanted so much to call out, but I was scared. He looked at me with anger in his eyes. "You really fucked up," he said and left the living room. I saw the key had been replaced in the deadbolt and in his absence, I tiptoed to the door and turned it. I was free. I didn't care about my car keys. I left the apartment and I ran. I didn't know where I was going, but I ran. My body ached and I didn't get far before I realized he was behind me, following me in my car. He was calling out to me, but I continued to run, until I came across an old man mowing his lawn. I tried to catch my breath to tell him what was going on, but my attacker got out of my car and walked away. He left my car there for me. I got in and sped off. I was heading back home.

Ω℥

I didn't report the attack to anyone accept Allen. Who would have believed me? Here I was a gay man, who freely visited someone I had met on the street. I could imagine how I would be perceived. It was my fault that I had placed myself in such a situation. I sure as hell would not receive sympathy from the police. So it was shared only with Allen.

When he returned I was happy to see him, but I also hated him. Had he stayed with me, this would have never happened. But it did. I explained to him what had happened and in his own way he offered support. He went with me to be tested for everything to make sure that I was, in his words, "clean."

For a while, I didn't want him to touch me. The thought of anyone putting a finger on me brought back memories of that night. The arms that I felt safe in were now extensions of this beast. I couldn't perform daily tasks, without looking behind me to see if he was following me. I was scared when someone snuck up behind me to say hello. I feared everything and everyone.

Allen's trips to Washington halted for a while as he attempted to take care of me. We would watch television until I fell asleep, but I would quickly awaken if I felt him reach out to me to get into bed. Although he tried his best to understand, he didn't. I couldn't share with him after our initial discussion what I was feeling. He was growing tired of it. And he showed it.

I started to drink a little more than usual to rid myself of the guilt and thoughts of that night. Allen was happy to drink with me, even smoke a little weed with me. This allowed me to numb all memories of that evening. In the past when we shared drinks and reefer, he knew that it would eventually lead to the two of us making love. This time it didn't. He leaned toward me after he placed the joint in the ashtray. He wanted to kiss, but I pushed him away. I was still scared.

He attempted to kiss me again and placed my hand on his hard dick. I told him I wasn't ready. He didn't care. He wanted to fuck and he wasn't going to wait anymore. He was tired of my "bullshit." I refused his advances, but not before he pulled his fist back and aimed it toward my face. I flinched, turning away, but not soon enough. His fist connected with my mouth, forcing me to taste the blood that was now flowing from my split lip. He grabbed me and threw me on the bed. I relived once again that night of horror.

After he finished, he saw the caked blood on my lip. He stroked my back and apologized. He told me he loved me and went to sleep. From that moment, he started a new trend in our relationship; he would hit me, fuck me, and then tell me he loved me.

I acknowledge that in the past, certain things I said or did got under his skin. I would argue to the point that Allen's anger escalated and it would play out in me receiving a black eye, or one of many busted lips. My body would absorb some of the bruises and punches; other times my face displayed his artwork. Between the fights and the numerous individuals he fucked in the same bed we shared, I continued to love him and I continued to allow him to love me the only way he knew how.

chapter nine

My mother's return to Richmond finally came during the time my senior year was in progress. She was not keen on the idea of me dating Allen, or any man for that matter. After meeting him, she took a liking to him. Although she was convinced he was a good guy, I knew that he wasn't. Along with the bruises, I'd dealt with catching Allen in bed with two of my best friends on separate occasions. There were rumors circulating that, of course, got back to me about his escapades, so I knew there were others. But my spirit and what love I had for myself had been beaten out of me, literally. I carried shame with me, like my driver's license. I attempted to disguise the pain I endured, but everyone saw it but me. We stayed together until the final beating.

I somehow managed to graduate from high school, not with my official graduating class, but with the other citywide rejects who had fucked up along the way during their senior year. My senior year saw me taking the remainder of the year off and finishing with the two classes I needed in summer school. I paid for that degree that summer but I still walked. Allen and I remained together and I continued to endure his beatings.

Shortly after graduation, my former high school drama teacher was doing a one-woman show to showcase her talents. I loved her like a second mom. In my own mother's absence, she stepped in, within boundaries, to provide some support. I could go to her and share with her my life without feeling ostracized. She, too, had met Allen and fallen prey to his charm.

He always told me that he wanted to see her perform. I was happy during this rare time of his interest. Our evenings usually consisted of arguing, fighting, fucking and making up. It was getting pretty old. But I sensed, or rather hoped, that since we were getting older, things would change. But they didn't.

I purchased tickets for his birthday to attend her performance. After a nice dinner, we walked around the giant performance center as I said hello to former teachers and classmates who came out to catch her performance. Allen lagged behind. I introduced him to everyone I knew and he begrudgingly greeted them. I couldn't understand this change of heart; it was his desire to see her perform that had led us here.

We took our seats for her performance. During her heartwarming portrayal of Madame C.J. Walker, he fell asleep. He started to snore a bit and I nudged him. He got up in the middle of her performance and walked out. He waited in the lobby until the show was over. As I left the orchestra seats I'd purchased for the two of us, I searched for him in the crowd. He was pissed.

We didn't really talk as we headed toward the car. Whatever was bothering him, I prayed would be resolved before it ruined this birthday treat for him. There was no resolution.

He hated the show. He thought it was boring as all hell and wanted to know why I had nudged him to wake up. I attempted to explain that he was snoring and the people close to us could hear him. He yelled at me for treating him to such a "shitty" show. As he continued to yell when we got in the car, he backhanded me in the mouth. That was it. I was tired of getting hit, only to hear "I love you" after sex. I was just hoping that the bruising wouldn't show since I now worked for a bank. When I got home, I immediately applied the remedies I had used so many times to prevent puffiness. Luckily when I woke up the next morning for work, I looked pretty okay.

We didn't speak for a week or so and I had resolved that the relationship was over. We had gone back and forth too many times over the last four years and it was getting us nowhere. I went to work as I did every day and came directly home.

৪৩৫৩

Tuesdays were cheap movie night at the local movie theater. You could catch a new release for the price of "Good Neighbor Hour" all evening. I had spent too much time, waiting and hoping for Allen to come around and see that I loved him. I didn't want a love that only showed its face in anger. I had cried wolf so many times on the drenched shoulders of friends, that they became frustrated when they saw the two of us together. I decided I wanted to get out that Tuesday and agreed to go to the movies with some co-workers. I decided to ride with one of the other two black guys in my department from work.

Right after I had committed myself to the movies, I received a call from Allen. He apologized profusely for his actions and wanted to know if we could get together to talk things out. I couldn't refuse him. Hell, I had spent four years with this man and in those four years, he did show me love at times.

He agreed to pick me up from the apartment my mother and I shared. We would go to the movies my co-workers were attending and then grab something to eat. He wanted to work things out. In the past, Allen had a way of canceling at the last minute, so I made backup plans with Rocky, my co-worker. And believe me, Allen didn't disappoint.

I showered and awaited his arrival as I had done many times waiting for my father growing up. I answered the phone on its second ring and heard Allen's voice. He had changed his mind. He wasn't coming over because he had made other plans. He had company and he even attempted to share with me who it was before I wished him a good evening and hung up. During the few moments it took me to call Rocky and give him directions to my house, Allen attempted to interrupt the call a number of times.

I heard Rocky pull up and headed out the door. We talked a little about work and the excitement of Spike Lee's latest film. Suddenly I noticed something. As we pulled out of the parking lot, right behind us in his work van, was Allen.

He sped up to catch the eye of Rocky and yell something to him. I hadn't come out to any of my male co-workers, especially Rocky. I was able to lie and say that Allen was someone dating my ex-girlfriend. Rocky was none the wiser; he couldn't make out what Allen was saying, but I had a pretty good idea.

He followed us in hot pursuit from the time we entered the acceleration ramp to hit the highway, until we arrived at the convenience store, just a stone's throw from the movie theater.

As we pulled into the parking lot, I looked around for Allen's van. I sighed a heavy relief, hoping he had decided against making a scene. But he hadn't. As Rocky entered the store, I heard a knock on the window.

I knew that look. I had seen it many times before. But this time, he decided to use his words to hurt me and not his fists. He tapped on the window and I asked him not to do anything. He had a twisted smile on his face, as he informed me of his plans. "I'm going to get even with you; not physically, but mentally." I couldn't comprehend why he wanted to do this; after all he was the one who had cancelled with me. As he spoke, Rocky came out of the store. They acknowledged each other with that head nod. "Wassup?" they said in unison.

If you have ever seen a deer caught in the headlights, that was the look on Rocky's face as Allen continued, "Did you know he was a punk? That's my boyfriend. What the fuck are you doing with him?" I sat there shocked. I looked both ways to see both of their reactions.

"Yo man, he is a co-worker of mine, I don't go that way," Rocky volleyed.

Allen caught his words on the edge of his racket and swatted back, "Are you going to fuck him tonight? 'Cause that's all he's good for is a good piece of ass." Game. Set. Match. And with that, Allen climbed into his vehicle and pulled off.

ဆာငအ

I arrived at work the next morning, as always 8:15 precisely. By nine o'clock everyone in my department knew that I was gay. I tried to apologize to Rocky but he was not having it. He was pissed that he was placed in such a situation, one that I never thought would happen. As the day continued, I could hear the mailroom guys outside my cubicle make comments about what happened and there was nothing I could do. Eventually, my supervisor called me into her office to tell me to stop talking about my lifestyle. But I hadn't said a word, someone else had.

Now some would say that I was stupid for taking him back after everything, but I did. I didn't know any better. I was a grown man, yet I was still acting like a child searching for love. Of all the men in my life, Allen was the only one who showed me any semblance of love, or what I perceived to be love. Although the four years had become an emotional roller coaster, he gave me more in those four years than my father ever had. We had to work it out. I couldn't stand losing someone else if I could prevent it.

I eventually lost him. I lost him to the newest face and the freshest piece of ass that stepped off the bus in Richmond. By this time, Allen was doing everything right once again. He started to be more caring, more patient, more understanding. All the while, he was weaving this spider web for me to become entangled. And I did just that. When I officially lost him, I also lost me.

Little did I know or want to believe, Allen was still sleeping with me and whispering sweet nothings in my ear at night. On the nights we were not together, he was doing the same with the new face from the Trailways bus depot. I thought to myself, *How fucking stupid can you be? How much more are you going to take?* I realized that I couldn't do it anymore.

৪৩৫৪

The final straw came one night Allen invited me over and to my surprise, his new piece was there. I know what sex smells like and it was lingering in the air. I felt so used and hurt that I decided to take matters into my own hands. For four years, I had allowed this man to build me, only to knock me down. I would come when he called, I would do anything for him. I lost myself once again and I didn't know how to find myself. Allen had made me fall in love with him all over again. As I smelled the lingering scent of Jergens and shit in the air, I knew this was the worst hurt he could ever inflict upon me.

I'd left the same boardinghouse room Allen and I shared with the two of them laughing at me. Yes, I had been a fool. My self-esteem was so shot that nothing mattered. I hadn't taken my suit off from work before I headed for the cupboard where I knew my mom stored alcohol. I grabbed the bottle of vodka she kept on hand for visitors and swallowed it. I felt the burn and satisfaction as it went down. It wasn't a smooth taste, nor was it enough to kill the pain of what I was feeling, but it made me courageous. I swallowed more of the bottle. I stumbled to the bathroom to retrieve a razor from the medicine cabinet. I didn't want my mother to catch me or find my bloody body, so I took the remaining vodka with me and got in my car.

The "Quiet Storm's" disc jockey always seemed to cater to your emotions, as he played the songs that fit your mood. I swerved, avoiding oncoming traffic, listening to the songs that once brought me joy and now brought sadness. At every stoplight, I found myself wiping my tears and drinking the contents of the bottle until it was empty. In my gray pin-striped suit, with a pink oxford and paisley tie, I felt like Clark Kent, but with the bottle I felt like Superman. When there was nothing left, I stopped at the red light. I looked at the razor blade I had taken from the medicine cabinet. It was resting beside me in the passenger's seat. I looked at the crimson light, stopping me from proceeding. I placed my car in park and looked over to the white girl staring at me from the passenger's seat in the next lane. She smiled. I couldn't. I darted my eyes from hers so that she couldn't see me. Within a matter of a few seconds, the next red I saw was the blood spurting from my opened wrists.

I woke up in the emergency room. My arms outstretched, bound by tape to prevent my movement. I felt the needle enter my wrist to stitch the gash I had created. They couldn't numb me anymore; they wanted me to feel what I had done. I looked at my blood-soaked suit, and while I lay there in excruciating pain, the only thought that entered my sobering mind was, *I hope my father does not get upset if and when he sees my suit.*

I stayed with my employer for a couple of years after my suicide attempt.

I never thought being gay would get me any further than the clerical job I had, but I was quickly promoted and transferred to Northern Virginia and eventually back to Baltimore. Allen was now a memory. Even though Baltimore was my introduction to the gay lifestyle, being there now had changed me as an adult. The few places I remembered from that time were now gone. I never saw Michael, Alex or Carol again and I felt alone. After a brief stay in Baltimore, I moved back to Richmond to regroup and decide what would be the next road on this journey.

chapter ten

I returned to Richmond and started working for City Hall. It was a gig. It paid the bills I had accumulated and that was it. I got no pleasure or joy out of it. I called people every day to find out why they didn't pay their bills. I really didn't care, but I had to. On occasion, I would see Allen. He was still with the guy he left me for and they were having their own set of issues. It was funny, because they sounded vaguely like the same issues he and I'd had. But I couldn't deal with his shit and mine at the same time. I was trying to figure out what to do with my own life and I clearly had no direction.

One of the guys Allen slept with during our four years together had moved to New York. Time had passed and healed that wound between the two of us. We were able to salvage the friendship. When he visited, he would share his stories of the Big Apple and his desire to make it on Broadway. Our relationship was a weird one. Although we were friends in high school, we had such a competitive relationship. I gave him his props; he was and is an incredible dancer. We competed for roles in high school productions. At one point, we even competed for the affections of the same man. But he always hated me because of my complexion. I remembered he stopped talking to me in class one day. When I asked why, he simply replied, "You think it's all about you because you are light-skinned." Did he know the hell that I was going through? Could he possibly imagine what it was like? He didn't know that I thought of my complexion as a hindrance more so than anything else. I envied his beautiful dark skin. We never discussed it again. He moved to New York and I was stuck in Richmond.

I decided after one of his visits that New York was the place for me. I started to do some research on job opportunities and apartments. At this time, I met an up-and-coming writer. After reading his first novel, I threw him a book signing here in Richmond with the help of one of the local African-American bookstores. From this newfound relationship, came a budding friendship. He would figure prominently in my relocation to New York. It was time to find my voice. There was nothing really holding me back in Richmond.

Growing up, I always wanted to be in the entertainment industry. I wanted to be the next Sidney Poitier. I wanted to entertain people. I must say I enjoyed the attention that was showered on me by family and friends alike. It brought joy to me being the center of attention. I would tell jokes to solicit laughter. I wanted to act. My goals at that time were to become the next African-American male to win an Oscar. They were dreams of a child who got lost in the old black-and-white movies that aired on Sunday afternoons. I never thought in a million years that I would ever get the opportunity to pursue it. Hell, Richmond seemed galaxies away from New York and it was not in the cards for me. But my writer friend heard my prayers.

෫෯ඏ

I attended New York's Gay Pride in June 1992. The writer had arranged a meeting with me and the president of the company conducting his public relations. I wanted to maximize my trip while there, so I found my way to the building on Seventh Avenue and entered.

For the next three hours, I interviewed. In between the telephones ringing off the hook, I met with both the president and vice president of this mom-and-pop PR company. Between the constant interruptions, he informed me about the job and the duties it entailed. Before I could ask the perfect follow-up question, he was interrupted again, by something or someone. I put on my best "Yes, Sirs" and "No, Ma'ams" to impress both him and his subordinate. He sized me up once or twice. During this painstaking interview, he informed me, that since I was from the South, people would take advantage of me. He continued, I would be fucked 2,000 times without Vaseline before I woke up and said ouch. But I had this dream that I wanted for so long, I could endure the pain. I did it the first time in Allen's backseat, so I was used to it, of course. I left the interview feeling good about it and my performance. I spent the remainder of my weekend enjoying the festivities of Gay Pride. Before I headed back to Richmond that Monday, I received the call, informing me the job was mine.

I moved to New York in August 1992. Before relocating, my high school competitor helped me find an apartment share in his building. He lived in 1-E and I was in 4-E. We had overcome the high school antics and it was great to have someone not only from home nearby, but in the same building. On my last day of work with City Hall, I loaded up a friend's car and we made the trip to New York. We stopped at the local rest stops along the New Jersey Turnpike because both of our bodies were tired from the weeklong day-to-day grind. Our sleep-deprived bodies came to life, as the morning greeted us. We continued through Manhattan by way of the West Side Highway, heading north toward my new home in Washington Heights.

It was a cool, rainy day that Saturday when we arrived. As we got off the exit, I couldn't help but think about my new surroundings. The grass I was used to seeing every day in Richmond, had now been replaced with cracked-concrete walkways. The bumpers of cars kissed one another, providing very little room to move if you were in a hurry. I found the apartment building that I would call home and thought to myself, *it ain't Richmond.*

I rang the buzzer of the apartment waiting to hear the voice of my new roommate. As I waited, knowing that he had already cashed my rent check and security deposit, I looked at the entry door that had been riddled with bullets. There were lights in the lobby, but because of the darkness of the floors and walls, it became suffocating. I heard the sleepy voice buzz us up. The elevator didn't work that day, so everything that I was able to move in the car, had to be walked up the never-ending flights of stairs.

I decided that I would purchase a bed once I moved to the city, rather than take anything big and bulky with me. My friend and I blew up the air mattress, stored everything else in the corner for the meantime, and after exchanging pleasantries with my new roommate, we crashed.

When I woke up, I looked around the huge room. It was very spacious. A good designer and available funds could create not only a sleeping area, but an entertainment area as well. I knew that wouldn't happen for me. I had such a desire to work in New York and live in New York that I'd accepted a job for slave wages. I agreed to a salary of $12,000, with the goal that once I established myself, I would move on. All I needed was the right venue to get my foot in the door.

I also agreed to pay the fee of $250 per month plus utilities and that is just what I got. I looked around and noticed the white walls were dingy from dirt and grime. The hardwood floors had not been swept or mopped probably since my roommate had first moved in. I ventured into the bathroom to relieve myself, only to see the mold and mildew everywhere. As much as I wanted to pack things up and head back to Richmond, I needed to take a chance.

I found a drug store that carried the necessary cleaning supplies to make not only my bedroom, but the bathroom that I would share and the kitchen habitable. The fumes from the cleaning products opened my chest, eventually leading to a cold a few days later, but it was most necessary. After some serious scrubbing, a few hours later, it was clean. Since it was Saturday, my buddy who served as chauffeur and mover, wanted to explore the Village. After another brief nap, we headed out to paint the town.

Our first stop was the local watering hole, Two Potato. We watched with glee the drag show and the hostess declaring all-out war on one of the drunken patrons heckling her. From there, we headed toward the corner of West Side Highway and Christopher Street to Keller's. Once I walked in, I realized that I would be spending a great deal of my time there. I liked it. It had the right combination of comfort and sleaze that satisfied all my cravings. Yes, New York, I had arrived.

After my friend left that Sunday afternoon, I spent a few minutes with my roommate getting instructions on how to ride the subway. I prepared my clothes for work and headed to bed, rather my air mattress. The last forty-eight hours had drained me and I didn't want to be late for my first day of work.

Preparations the night before my first day didn't help. After stepping off the train, I got so turned around trying to find the exit, I found myself on the opposite end of where I was supposed to be. With the help of a stranger, I found my way to work and headed upstairs to my new venture.

₧₨

I was immediately put to work answering the telephone. The gentleman who I interviewed with had not yet arrived and since I was going to be serving as his assistant, they wanted to keep me busy until he showed. I politely picked up the telephone, took the message and set it aside for him. I searched for other things to do until he arrived. I was pretty sure that he would want to spend some time with me to go over everything.

He breezed in the door, some four hours after I'd arrived. He walked past me without saying hello. I heard him call his colleague into his office and question who I was. She informed him that he had hired me to be his assistant and that he needed to let me know his expectations. That day was indicative of the days that would follow. Outside of being scolded and belittled by him, my direction came from his right-hand person. I had bought into this fantasy of working in the entertainment industry and didn't realize it was going to be so much work.

I eventually got used to his lack of communication and his cold demeanor, not only toward me, but others in the office. I would arrive early to work to type his memos that he'd left for me the previous night. He would provide me with handwritten letters that really made no sense whatsoever. His handwriting was illegible and difficult at times to decipher, but I was going to make this work. I wanted to.

I really didn't have much of a social life. I did go out on occasion with my high school friend who helped me find the apartment and another friend of ours Jim, who had recently relocated to New York. I spent more time with Jim because he wasn't working and had more free time on his hands.

On the rare occasions that I had the energy to do something on the weekends, Jim and I would hang out at the local watering holes in the Village, hoping that someone would buy us a drink because we didn't have two pennies to rub between the two of us.

Work became consuming and as it did, I learned more and more. I learned when my boss was in a good mood and when he wasn't. I learned how he liked his coffee, so if I had extra money from the meager wages, I would have the brewing cup on his desk with his numerous letters and proposal for his review. I tried to stay one step ahead of the game. As I found my footing, he softened just a little bit, but not too much. There were still days when I tried to figure out whether he was on his rag or the women around me. I educated myself on everyone's cycle.

I was able to cope with the shit at work—that's what I was hired to do— but I wanted to make more time for me. When I found myself needing a connection to home, I would visit Jim after work and we would sit there and reminisce of home. He would allow me some of his time even though he didn't work. He was afforded this luxury of unemployment due to the many suitors who provided monetary compensation for his time. Not that he was sleeping with these individuals; they found his conversation, like me, very soothing and warm.

I started to like New York a lot. Not really loving it, but liking it enough. I started to use my time wisely to make connections with others in the business. I didn't make a lot of money, $12,000 before taxes to be exact, so the friendships I established with others were folks at record labels who would mail me the latest musical releases. With some of the friendships came free movie premiere passes and front-row concert tickets. I had started tricking with a brotha I called the Yankee Slugger, because he lived in the Bronx and waved a big bat; but relationships, I had soured on them since Allen. The Yankee Slugger was there when I needed him. If I wanted to get fucked, he was just a phone call away. I knew he wanted more, but my heart was so hardened, all I could offer was a warm spot to fuck.

Jim had more free time on his hands to explore the city. When we were fortunate to have spare spending money after bills, he was able to take me to places I had not visited since I moved to the city.

One Saturday night after a long work week, and a pay week at that, Jim dragged me out. As we rode the subway to the Village, he informed me what the evening had in store for us. We were going to visit his friend Dan for a moment. Dan had arranged for Jim to meet a date there. I knew Dan and didn't particularly care for him. He was one of those queens who would look down on anyone not like him. He never told his real age, but you could tell from the scars located behind his ears, that he had been pulled and tucked.

Dan had a great apartment located in the heart of the Village. Once you ascended the many stairs to his apartment, you were greeted with enormous space, something rare in New York, even rarer in the Village. After climbing, both Jim and I were sweating. Unfortunately with the space, Dan didn't have central air conditioning. After the obligatory hellos, we sat around having a drink waiting for Jim's date. Time flew by. One good thing came out of it; I knew I wouldn't have to spend extra money that evening trying to get my drink on. But, I was getting a little pissed. Being a Virgo, I am a stickler for timeliness and this man was late. I looked at Jim and on my face; he knew it was time to go. I wasn't going to spend a nice evening sticking around for some dick that I didn't have a date with, even if the drinks were free.

We said good-bye to Dan and descended the stairs. You had to be extra careful because they were so steep. I kept my hand on the railing and my eyes carefully glued to my feet, watching carefully each step I took. Jim's ranting about my patience fell on deaf ears as I continued to focus on the task of getting the hell out of the building and into the streets. I continued to take each step slowly until I was blocked.

My eyes panned up from the well-worn cowboy boots, meeting the faded jeans, covered by a three-quarter-length jacket. As I approached this stranger's face slowly, I heard his voice. "Good evening." Balancing myself, I made eye contact with him. It was Jim's date and my future lover. His name was Thomas.

He quickly apologized to Jim as he searched out my face and I did the same in return. This was strange, I thought, for Jim to be going out with a black man, but whatever floated his boat, who was I to judge. His face was ruggedly handsome and he had a smile that stretched coast to coast, show-casing his pearly whites. I changed my mind and made my way back up the stairs so that Jim could talk with him. Actually, I had selfish reasons; I wanted to survey him again to make sure the trek back upstairs was worth it.

We re-entered Dan's apartment and while Jim and Thomas talked, Dan and I pretended that we actually cared what the other had to say. All the while I was checking Thomas out. I felt like a snake, but I liked what I liked. He was beautiful. He had a voice that women would throw their panties at him with a simple hello.

Before Jim and I left this time, the two of them agreed to meet at a later date. I shook his hand and felt the firm callous hand grab mine. I honestly have to admit I got an immediate hard-on. There was something so manly about him, that I felt like a little bitch. When he said good night, I was ready to take my drawers off and throw them at him.

Needless to say, it didn't work out with Jim and Thomas. After a second date, Jim realized Thomas was not right for him. I feigned disappointment in my dear friend not finding romance, but rejoiced silently to myself. I continued to question Jim why it didn't work out, hoping that he could provide me with an answer that would dissuade me from exploring something with Thomas. Jim informed me, although he liked Thomas, his endowment was a bit intimidating. That's all I needed to hear.

Jim would only go so far to the line with a guy. But I enjoyed sex and by this time my well was running dry, with the Yankee Slugger and I being on the outs. My options were limited in terms of sexual partners. I asked Jim's permission to contact Thomas. He gave me the go-ahead, but he wasn't going to make it easy for me. He refused to give me the number, nor would he give Thomas my number. If I wanted to meet up with Thomas, I would have to go through his best friend, Dan. Shit.

Well, I bit the bullet, ate a little humble pie and called Dan. Once again, I faked interest in his stories; he had information I needed. I expressed my interest to hook up with Thomas for a date and much to my surprise, Dan informed me that Thomas also had inquired about me. I gave Dan all of my contact numbers, including work, to pass on to Thomas. A couple of weeks later, I received the first of many calls.

ɛꙩભ

Because I spent so much time at work, that was the best place for Thomas to reach me. Between fielding calls for information from media outlets regarding the clients and fielding calls from my boss' creditors, I was able to talk to Thomas. When my boss had his ass on his back, he closed all doors between me and the rest of the staff to let me know my place as a peon. I was happy to be disconnected from the staff; it allowed me to speak freely with Thomas when he called.

After the initial call, Thomas and I spent the next two to three weeks learning each other. I gave him my 411 on being relatively new to New York and he told me what he wanted me to know, which wasn't a lot. He worked as a manager for a grocery store and I thought, how very blue collar, thus the calloused hands. I thought the mix would work well. We agreed to meet one night after I got off work, but of course, I had to work late for the overseer. I wasn't sure I would be able to make it. But I learned where there is a will, there is a way. Besides, I was kind of horny.

There are a couple of things that gay men have in common with women. One is hair. There is nothing like a good haircut or style to make one feel extra good about themselves. Two days before my arranged date with Thomas, I was selected to appear in a national hip-hop publication focusing on African Americans in the entertainment industry who worked behind the scenes. I was the low man on the totem pole where I worked, but that Southern charm worked well in securing me a spot in the photo shoot and magazine. They wanted me to have a different look, outside the conservative administrative assistant I had become.

I was pampered. I spent the morning having my hair twisted. I looked good, if I do say so myself. This new hairstyle gave me an air of confidence and yes, a little cockiness. I had a stylist select clothing for me from the Karl Kani clothing line and I felt hot for the first time in a mighty long while. I was instructed by the hairstylist to tie my hair up every night before bed so that it would keep. I immediately ran out and purchased a scarf.

The other thing that gay men have in common with women is the perfect outfit. Women have a tendency to spend a great deal of time selecting the right outfit to impress a man.

I spent the night before my date with Thomas choosing an outfit that would complement my new hairstyle. I agreed that the black-and-white-striped pants I had purchased in college that flared when I walked, worked well with a friend's hand-painted original gray vest over a white T-shirt. To set everything in motion, I wore a black-and-gray blazer to allow the outfit to pop. I was a walking contradiction in patterns.

I made my way up to Eighty-First and Amsterdam where I had agreed to meet Thomas. The bar was scarcely occupied as the sounds of John Leguizamo blared from the television monitors. I was late and hoped that I had not missed this opportunity. I looked around for the man with the golden voice. Everyone pretty much looked the same. I grabbed a Coke to settle myself and quench my thirst. Where was he, I thought. Did he stand me up? Feelings of my father's late arrivals and no-shows started to creep into my thoughts. I decided to focus my energy on the insane characters from John Leguizamo's show. I made my way to the bathroom just to check myself out one more time and wipe my brow. Although there weren't too many patrons, the bar felt very humid. As I went to push the door to the men's room open, there he was.

I had apologized so many times for things that I had no control over. Hell, I just liked apologizing and this was no exception. This man that stood in front of me had walked past me a number of times throughout the course of the evening. I realized that I had not recognized him from our first meeting. He accepted my apologies and we made our way to the bar. It was $1 marguerita night and happy hour was almost over. We sat watching the end of the comedy special, exchanging conversation and smiles. After the second or third drink, Thomas acknowledged that he didn't recognize me because of the new hairstyle. I laughed and turned the tables on him by making the same confession. He was wearing a baseball cap this evening. From our first encounter back at Dan's I knew he was folically challenged. We both laughed at this simple fact, not because it was extremely funny, but the cheap margueritas were beginning to work on us.

The evening continued and happy hour ended. We switched from the $1 drinks to the more potent Long Island Iced Teas. He took the lead and ordered rounds and rounds of drinks for us. I sized him up in his bib overalls, unbuttoned at the waist to show the black form-fitting boxers with the Calvin Klein brand name showing. His T-shirt contoured his chest and I peeked closer to see if Jim had told the truth about his manhood. I couldn't see, but it wasn't because I wasn't trying.

I felt like Cinderella at the ball. I did not want the evening to end, but I knew that it had to. I knew that my wicked stepmother was waiting in the form of my boss, and I didn't want to break my track record of getting to work early and preparing the day's events. I also realized that I was drunk and I didn't have money to take a cab home. I looked at Thomas and shared my dilemma with him: should I stay or should I go? If I were to stay, we would continue drinking and I was not good at holding my liquor. If I were to leave, would he go with me?

He answered my question as we made our way to the subway to take the A-train to my apartment. He was a perfect gentleman, holding me up and helping me through the turnstile toward the platform. I knew it was late because of the few riders on the platform heading uptown. My head was swimming from the toxic mix of alcohol and I felt my stomach turn a couple of times, but I didn't care. Thomas allowed me to lean on him as we waited for the train. I knew this late in the evening, it was going local and not express; I wanted to hurry up home and rest my thoughts, but also to tie my hair up before I passed out.

As I leaned on his shoulder, his head stood erect as he whispered, "Why don't you suck my dick right here?" I chuckled at the thought and passed it off as if I overheard a conversation I shouldn't have. But he asked again. I removed my head from his shoulder and looked into his bloodshot eyes. I mumbled in disbelief; there were too many people around. "No one is watching," he said, trying to convince me to step out of my comfort zone. I slowly scanned the platform and realized that it was no longer rush hour and we were two of only a handful waiting. I thought about it. I wanted this man and as his eyes followed me slowly down to his zipper, I took him out and took him in.

It only lasted a few brief moments, due to the noise of the oncoming train.

As we boarded the first car of the subway, Thomas noticed there were very few passengers on the train. *Where was everybody*, I thought. He repeated his earlier request and I willingly obliged while our few fellow passengers looked on, some in disbelief, others silently rooting.

We both stumbled to my apartment door. I searched the key ring to find the right one. Since I arrived in New York, I had never been this drunk. The Yankee Slugger had only been here once. Each time we fucked, it was at his place in the Bronx. Although not far from where I lived, for me going to the Bronx was like going to another town. I had never invited anyone else to come over. I figured who would want to head up to 172nd Street for sex, when you could go to any backroom in any of the city's gay bars and get a blowjob. Besides, I didn't particularly like the apartment. I tried to maintain the upkeep so that if a situation like this ever presented itself, at least my room and the bathroom were clean.

We made our way into my bedroom. I didn't want to turn on the bright ceiling light because I was pretty sure it would fuck me up even more. So I reached for the nightlight I had purchased and plugged it into the socket. It illuminated the room with just enough light to see him. He rested on his elbows on the edge of the bed, allowing me kneeling access to his crotch that I savored on both the platform and the train. I continued where I'd left off. I felt him growing in my mouth, but I quickly stopped. I realized I needed to do something first. I excused myself and grabbed what I needed and headed toward the bathroom. When I returned, Thomas had removed his bib overalls allowing me more access and I had completed what I had left the room for: to tie up my hair.

I didn't know what it was that was so intriguing about this man or this moment. I found myself excited at the thought of being intimate, as I fought back the gagging that I was experiencing. Jim was right. Actually, Jim's description had done Thomas no justice. As I continued, the heat of the room intensified my already intoxicated thoughts. I attempted to deep-throat Thomas and his glorious friend and realized that it was not possible. I had hit a point where I needed to stop. I excused myself again. This time I visited the bathroom, I called Earl, the porcelain God.

I wiped my mouth and gargled. My head was throbbing and I realized that I had not eaten. When I returned to the room to figure out what to do next, Thomas was dressed. He excused himself for the evening, stating that it was getting late and he needed to get up early in the morning. As I locked the door behind him, I thought, this blows and not in a good way.

I spent the next day at work sucking back ice-cold Coca-Cola and Tylenol to control the throbbing and pounding headache from the previous night. I shared with my girlfriend Kay the events that led to my tremendous hangover. She had become a wonderful friend after our initial meeting. With her beautiful brown eyes, she laughed at me as I told her everything, well, with the exception of a few parts. I figured that I wouldn't hear from Thomas after he saw me so drunk. I was still horny, so I decided to schedule a meeting with the Yankee Slugger. As I went through my Rolodex to retrieve the Slugger's number, the telephone rang. It was Thomas.

I met Thomas downstairs from my office as I headed to retrieve another Coke from the local bodega. He laughed at my actions from our night of drinking. He thought it was cute, I thought otherwise. He was on his way to his second job and wanted to check on me to make sure I was okay. After seeing me in all my wonderful glory, he agreed that we should try it again, however, next time we wouldn't consume as much as we did. It hurt to smile as he walked away, but I looked forward to seeing him soon.

Thomas and I met that Sunday morning for coffee. We rehashed the events that led me to call Earl on our first date. As I watched him, his smile was even bigger and brighter than I had remembered. You could almost count every tooth in his mouth and after watching closely, you could tell he took much care in keeping that smile white. We walked around a bit and headed back to my apartment.

My roommate wasn't home that afternoon and we decided to watch a little television before he headed to work. I didn't have a chair or sofa in my bedroom, so the bed I recently purchased served as both. He lay back on the bed, propping himself up on his arms as I sat on the edge. I was a little nervous this time because I had no liquid courage. He took his foot and rubbed my back. When I turned to look back at him, with a simple head nod, he invited me to join him at the head of the bed. He rested his head on his arm, as he held me in the other. I placed my hand on his chest and laid my head there for comfort. Oh, it felt so good. I knew the dream would be interrupted with the reality of him having to work later that evening, but I closed my eyes and enjoyed the moment.

Our bodies shifted as he removed his hand from behind his head and pulled me closer to kiss him. I had always closed my eyes when I kissed in the past, but I noticed that we both were staring at each other as we kissed. He placed me on my back and placed his body atop mine. He managed to take both my hands in his and place them behind me as he continued to kiss me. I felt his body press into mine and I reciprocated. Holding both my hands with just one of his, he slowly undressed me. First, unbuttoning my shirt. His hands then slid down to my jeans, unbuttoning them just to allow his hands to caress my waist.

I took his lead and reversed our positions. I removed my shirt completely as he lay there. With him now on his back and me on my knees, I picked up where we started the last time we were on the subway platform. I felt him harden. I allowed him to slip out of my mouth and heard the thud as it hit his stomach. I removed his boots and jeans. Before I could continue, he reached into his pocket to the get the bottle of poppers. Okay, I guessed he knew what he wanted when he came here.

By now, we were both naked. Our mouths were exploring each other's bodies, moist from the city's humidity. My apartment was old, so there was no central air conditioning. The box fan I purchased provided no cooling relief, just the continued circulation of hot air. The taste of his body was a combination of sweetness and salt. I lapped at every available spot and enjoyed the mixture of flavors. I had never experienced the taste of a man's ass and I dared not venture into areas foreign to me, nor did I enjoy some-one eating my ass. But Thomas' skillful tongue drove me crazy, as he pushed my legs back to expose to him what he wanted. I felt his tongue slide in slowly, opening me up and teasing me. I had wanted this since I first met him. My head tossed from side to side. I moaned more and more, as he continued to explore my insides with his tongue.

When he felt me relax, he reached into his pocket again for a condom and the little lube packs every bar in town had on display. He took note of my semi-tightness and allowed more than enough lubrication to saturate and prepare me. I raised my head to see him apply the remainder to his stiff shaft. I turned to find the bottle of poppers I knew I would need for this joyride.

I took a deep breath after inhaling the burning poppers. I reached for Thomas, noticing that he was pressing against the entrance. As my body calmed I guided him in slowly. Although I was used to getting fucked, Thomas was larger than I had expected. I felt his head enter me. My body initially rejected him because of the pain I felt, but I wanted him. The Yankee Slugger had nothing on Thomas. He was gentle as I continued to guide him in after a moment of hesitation. I winced, feeling the expansion. I took another hit of the poppers, waiting for the intrusion to end. It felt like it would never stop.

He rested for a moment, allowing me to get situated. I thought, *oh my God, it's all in.* I didn't know how it was possible, but I was glad that I could be accommodating. With slow, rhythmic motions, he teased me. I felt my muscles tighten around him as he stretched me out. He was patient. I knew from his workout, that he was an experienced lover and he made me feel every inch of his precision.

He wrapped my legs around his waist and leaned forward to kiss me. He held me close as he pumped slowly, stopping at times when he felt my body ready to force him out again. His arms held me tight as he continued. He was not only going in and out, but this time he circled the globe. My body was experiencing pleasures that I had never thought were possible.

I felt his sweat drop from his face onto me as he increased his speed. He was careful not to hurt me. He wanted to make it pleasurable. But some-thing was wrong. I couldn't figure out what it was. I was searching for answers as I shuddered several times. I arched my back, meeting his every thrust, feeling something I had never felt before. I couldn't make heads or tails of this pain I was feeling, shooting from the small of my back, hit-ting every nerve and tingling every part of my body. I tried to fight the thoughts, but I couldn't. I reached my hands behind Thomas to bring him closer to me, deeper in me and each time, I felt this jolt of pleasure increase. He must have noticed that my eyes had rolled back in my head and he slowed down, but it was too late. I pulled him deeper inside one last time, tightening the grip I had on him with my thighs and for the first time, I came without touching myself.

He reached his moment shortly after I did and slowly removed himself. I turned away from him, refusing his touch as I tried to gather my thoughts. I shivered, even in the hot thickness of the air, and pushed his hands away as I tried to catch my breath. I closed my eyes and the fight in me left, as he once again, silently reached for me and held me. I cried. It is sad to say, now that I look back, that that's all it took to realize that I was in love.

chapter eleven

I blossomed after that Sunday afternoon with Thomas. Nothing that my boss said or did bothered me. I had a new skip in my step and work became more and more tolerable. I knew that when the day was over, I would see Thomas. Nothing else mattered. Kay even noticed a change in my attitude and behavior. She pointed out that there was a change in me that she couldn't quite put her finger on. I knew that she knew, and she knew that I knew she knew what it was, but we never discussed it. We would smile across from each other and it was all good.

By this time, my boss had decided to give me a chance at doing publicity. Initially, I thought it was a demotion from having his ear every day as his assistant, but I didn't care. Let somebody else deal with his shit. I had learned from watching Kay how to be a great publicist. She had taught me how to write press releases and bios, and she had even taught me how to find something redeeming in a group or performer that you didn't necessarily like or agree with.

I rushed through the days at work and even some late-night events with professionalism and courtesy. I was always working something or someone to bring in business. I didn't care that when I got home there was barely enough to eat in the cupboards. I was living the life I had always dreamed, I was making things happen in the industry for groups I was assigned, and most importantly, I was in love.

Things only got better with Thomas. Because we worked different schedules, I robbed myself of sleep to greet him when he made his way to see me during the wee hours of the morning. I would compensate for it when I got home from work. I would nap, catching up on the missed eight hours. When he arrived, he usually carried a bag or two of groceries to offset my limited income. We would sit there, smoking a little pot, watching late-night info-mercials and end the night making love. My body ached for him, for his touch.

Sometimes when he was off, he would meet me after work and we would hang out and drink. I had learned my lesson from our first date and recognized my limitations. We explored bars on the East Side and in Alphabet City, which offered more colorful characters than the ones I was used to in the West Village. After tossing back a few, we would find a little bodega or all-night pizza place, grab something to eat, and hightail it back to my place. We never went to his place. I never once questioned why, until he had me hooked.

One night after bar hopping and drinking, I was all prepared to do our usual. Grab something to eat, leave, and go back and fuck. But this night was different. After we ate, I noticed that Thomas grabbed a couple of extra slices of pizza and had them wrapped to go. I thought it strange that he would ask for more when he had just devoured the semi-hot pizza to coat our stomachs. I asked why he needed more and he told me. The pizza to go was for his ex-lover—the ex-lover who lived with him.

My jaw dropped at this revelation. Thomas assured me that we would discuss it further as he hailed a cab for me to make sure I made it home safely. Fuck. Just when I thought everything was good in my life, I was thrown a curveball. I barely rested that night as I anticipated the next day's conversa-tion and figured where I fell in the scenario.

When we met the next day after I got off work, I had taken the night and the balance of the day to frame the questions I had for him. As we waited for our order, the tension was growing, as neither one of us wanted to begin the conversation. After moments of silence, he broke the hush.

Thomas informed me that his ex lived with him due to financial and health reasons. Before I could get out my first question, he quieted me with the rest of his story. The puzzled look on my face told him I needed to know more. Why hadn't he told me this before I invested my heart into this relationship? I received the response that all of us have heard in the past. "Well, there's nothing going on between us." But for me, that wasn't good enough. Up until this point, I never once knew where he lived. I'd only heard of the area Gramercy Park when we initially met. I fished for more and more answers, but those I received were guarded. I had a choice in the matter—continue or let go. I threw caution to the wind and trusted him. I was experiencing a love unlike before. I didn't want to risk losing him because of my insecurities, but I need to know more. I needed to know for my own peace of mind.

Before this surprise, I had never questioned where Thomas was when he wasn't with me. I knew while I was at work, he was home resting so he could go to work when I ended my work day. He had given up his daytime job for the moment, leaving the door open for a future return. We saw each other just about every night, but those moments when he had other things to do, I started to question what was going on.

Over drinks at one of our many hangouts, I needed him to tell me. I knew from his words and his gifts that he loved me, but I wanted to know more about him; where he lived in this area he referred to as Gramercy Park. I was not going to let it rest. I needed peace of mind. Because of the living arrangements with him and his ex, I promised that I would not visit until he invited me. How fucking stupid I was. I knew nothing about the East Side and now I realized I knew less and less about the man I loved. I needed to know where he went every night that he wasn't with me.

When someone darts their eyes from you when they speak, remember one thing: They are lying.

He provided me with a street address. With that information, he also provided me with a false sense of security. I logged the information into my mental database until I needed it for future reference.

I was assigned more established artists to represent at work and continued to breeze along in promoting them. One day, my boss blew up at me and I was fed up. I looked at Kay after I exited his office, getting what little ass I possessed chewed off and said, "I'm outta here." I had never taken a lunch hour before, outside of running downstairs to grab a sandwich to eat at my desk, but I needed some fresh air to clear my thoughts. I found myself making my way to the subway, heading in the direction of Gramercy Park. The only way I could contact Thomas was at work and I knew he would not be there for another couple of hours.

I followed the directions given to me by the token booth operator. I walked up the stairs heading toward East Twenty-Third Street to find my man and tell him how rough of a day I was having. I walked the long blocks searching for the address that he had given me. I crossed the street to see if the building he referred to was there. I went as far as turning the corners, remembering that sometimes the address was not actually on the corner they were assigned. I stood there. I would not find Thomas that day, nor would I find the address he had given me. It didn't exist.

I felt sick as I made my way back to work. I couldn't help but think how much of a fool I was. I couldn't share this bit of information with Kay or anyone else, because I didn't want them to tell me how stupid I was. I already knew that. I found myself replaying moments of deception from Michael and Allen. I allowed Kay to field my calls as I tried to focus on what I needed to say to Thomas when I saw him.

"I knew you would do that, that's why I gave you the wrong address," he said over dinner when he arrived at my apartment. What? How could he say something like that? Yes, I did it, not because I was being nosey, but I was having a rough day and I wanted to see him to offer me some sort of comfort and support. He wouldn't look at me because he was upset at my "betrayal," as he put it.

I sat there and recoiled, feeling like that little boy scolded by his father. I asked, "If something were to happen to me, how could I contact you? How could anyone at work contact you to let you know something was wrong?" Because I had violated his trust, it would take a while for him to reveal the truth to me. I was wrong for what I'd done. As he rolled off me later that night, I felt like shit.

I was given a pager number a few days later to contact him if there was an emergency. This was my one and only direct connection to him, outside of his work number. Again, I allowed myself to settle for what he gave me because I needed it. I had lost all sense of self-pride and self-preservation. I needed to be cool and play the game his way because he created the rules. I willingly obliged.

Our relationship, as with any other relationship, had its ups and downs. If we argued or disagreed, Thomas knew how to punish me. The calls I made to him at work were answered by someone else saying he was busy. Knowing what time he left, I would wait until he was ready to close up shop. When I called back, I would be told that I had just missed him. He refused to return my pages until he felt I was in control of my feelings or when he wanted to be with me. It was very cruel. When we did connect and everything was all right, I felt on top of the world. He had introduced me to cocaine and on occasion, I would snort it with him at his urging to prolong our lovemaking. I became addicted, not to the cocaine, but to him.

In my heart I knew that I would spend the rest of my life with him. There were things we needed to work out, but for the first time, I had found someone that I could love. I was fooling myself. Every now and then those insecurities tapped me on the shoulder when I would see Thomas look at someone else while we were out, or saw someone flirting with him. When this took place, I stepped back to avoid confrontation.

I needed to do something to hold on to him. I didn't want to risk losing him as I did Allen to a new face, a tighter ass. We had been consistently using condoms during our lovemaking, but I wanted to truly show my devotion to him and the love we shared, or thought we did. Before he reached for the condom to make love one night, I shook my head no. I trusted him. We never used a condom again.

There were times during our moments of intimacy that we made love. But there were also times we just fucked. It was the kind of sex that had you hurting and in pain when it was over, but craving so much more. I enjoyed it, although I was sore until he wanted to do it again.

One night after lying in bed after an all-out session, Thomas said something that would change my life. It was in the summer season and I wasn't feeling well. I didn't have health coverage through my job, so I had to forego a couple of bills to pay to go see a doctor. I was diagnosed with strep throat. There was a possibility that I had been exposed to hepatitis but after a second round of blood work, it was determined I was negative.

His back was turned to me as he lit his cigarette. "How long have you been HIV positive?" he said, exhaling the smoke that filled his lungs. I was shocked at such an allegation. I remembered vividly being tested before the move to New York and my results were negative. He eventually turned back around to focus his attention on the television. I couldn't believe that he presumed that I would not have told him I was positive, if in fact I was. He continued to smoke, ignoring what I was feeling. He turned to retrieve the ashtray and place it on his lap.

"How could I not tell you something like that, if it was true," I said. "We haven't been using condoms and I know who and what I have been doing." I broke down and started to cry as I had many times behind him.

He offered no sympathy. "You have all the symptoms of someone who is," he said as he butted his cigarette. I tried to figure out where this was coming from and he offered no answers from his distracted look. I asked him to believe me, but his focus was not on me. I told him, actually insisted, that we both get tested if we were going to continue to fuck without a rubber. I turned over holding my pillow as I cried, muffling my sounds of hurt. He reached for me and apologized. He forced me to face him and without missing a beat, forced me on my back and eased himself back into me.

chapter twelve

Fall rolled around and it was the beginning of the end for quite a few of my friends. I received a call from my mother informing me that a dear friend had died. I made a call to a friend who had introduced me to "Almaz," a beautifully haunting song by Randy Crawford. I shared with him that the artist I was representing did a cover version of the song he had introduced me to. He, in return, informed me that another friend had succumbed.

When Thomas and I met for dinner, heading out for New Jersey, I shared with him my recent loss. We hadn't discussed being tested again since the night he had asked if I were positive. He was more focused on his own personal thoughts that he elected to keep to himself. I posed the question to him, "Would you ever tell me if you were positive?" I figured that if either of us had been exposed, it would have manifested itself in some form by now. He looked at me with a chillingly cold stare and said, "No, I wouldn't tell you."

As September came to a close, Thomas decided that he needed a break from me. It was as if it came out of left field. There was nothing I could do or say to convince him that we were meant to be together. For every point I made, there was a counterpoint. I thought back to his comments the night that I told him that my friend had died. He told me he would simply walk away from me if he were positive. And he did just that. He walked away.

With Thomas now out of the picture, I found myself without the much needed groceries or additional cash he provided to supplement my income. The company I worked for fell on hard times, often making payroll difficult to receive. I had bills coming out of my ass and had no one to turn to. My mother provided care packages that she sent once a month, which eventually became more frequent. I spent more time at home because I needed to save what money I had to get back and forth from work. Times were hard.

One night when Jim wanted to go out, he convinced me that he would foot the bill for that night's fun. I went out with him, but felt less jovial than our previous outings. It was no fun hanging out when you were at the mercy of someone else's dollar. Although I had carried Jim before, I felt like a leech. He still hadn't found a job, but he was doing much better than me.

∞∞

While we sat at the bar, Jim batted his eyes at unsuspecting conquests. He would purchase my drinks for me and have others who burned holes in his crotch from their stares to purchase his. While he carried conversations to secure one or two more drinks for himself, I would peruse the numerous free gay publications. I figured that maybe there were gay-owned businesses in the area and I could find some type of part-time work to offset some of the numerous bills.

I came across an advertisement for male escorts. It stated in bold lettering, one could make as much as $175 per hour, escorting men to functions throughout the city. There was no mention of sex or the possibilities of it in the ad. I figured I wasn't too hard on the eyes and maybe it was something that I could do to pay off a few bills in the meantime. I pocketed the publication and decided desperate times called for desperate measures.

I made the telephone call to the agency after weighing the decision. I arranged to meet the owner of the service at my apartment after playing phone tag. Before he arrived, he explained to me the service and wanted to make sure that I understood the possibilities that maybe, just maybe, sex was involved. He informed me this was not in the ad for editorial reasons. I needed the money and there was no end in sight to the accumulating bills.

"Degrading" is the only word that comes to mind when I think of the "interview." I was asked over the phone before the arranged meeting if I was a top, bottom or versatile. When I stated that I was versatile, the proprietor informed me, as part of the interview, I would have to bottom for him in order for him to feel secure in my abilities to "take dick" from potential clients. I prepared myself that evening before he arrived. Because Thomas and I fucked so much, I had invested in a personal cleaning device, to ensure that I didn't have any accidents when he penetrated me. There was nothing nastier than releasing your bowels during penetrative sex. So I retrieved the device to prepare for my interview. I plugged in the nightlight because I didn't want him to see my face clearly when he arrived. I felt I could get through it if I didn't have to see him as well.

I answered the knock on the door. He entered, carrying with him a file folder containing the rules and regulations of being an escort. Before providing me with a copy of the guidelines, he asked a series of questions for my "file." After the questions, he removed a tape measure from his pocket and proceeded to instruct me to get my dick hard. I closed my eyes to think of Thomas, but maintaining a hard dick for someone you are not interested in was difficult. It stayed hard long enough for him to get the correct measurements of length and girth. He raised the tape measure to my waist and chest for his records also. He looked at my body as I stood there naked and continued to hand me a list of do's and don'ts. I was hoping the list was longer than it was because I knew what would happen next. I lay there on my back and closed my eyes. I gave the greatest performance of my life.

It didn't last long, just long enough for him to check on his list that I could bottom. He wiped himself with the requested washcloth and told me he would be in contact. After Thomas and the Yankee Slugger, there wasn't much that he could do. Before I could hear him push the button for the elevator, I found myself in the shower, scrubbing off the scent of him and trying to wash away the shame I felt.

A few days later, New York was getting its first taste of winter with a light dusting of snow. I entered my cold apartment and retrieved the mail left behind for me by my roommate. I entered my bedroom to warm up by the space heater and noticed the red blinking indicator from my answering machine. I got the message to call the escort service for my very first job. The owner informed me he had a client in town from Atlanta who was house sitting and wanted someone Puerto Rican. I never denied my heritage as being a black man, nor did I think I could pull off being "Puerto Rican"-like, but the hour would pay me $125 and I could really use the money.

I showered and reached for the sample outfit I had received as part of the photo shoot I had participated in. I struggled with the thought of giving my body to someone who didn't care about me. For me, there had to be some type of connection, whether it was physical or emotional, for me to give my body away, but this was different, this was a necessity.

As I made my way to the address given to me, I thought about the man I would be servicing. I only knew he was from Atlanta and his name. I had never been to Atlanta a day in my life, but I knew folks from the Southern gay hub. With the name, it narrowed down individuals and my gut told me I knew my john for the evening.

I hit the buzzer to the apartment building, remembering my conversation with my "pimp." "Something tells me I know this person," I'd said to him, hoping with all hopes that it wasn't who I thought it was. "Well, it's your choice to take the call or not. I need to know now." I took the call.

As the elevator reached the fifteenth floor, I made a right and headed down the long hallway searching out the apartment number. I reached the second door to my left and knocked on the door. I rang the doorbell and hung my head low, so that whoever was behind the door could not see the fear in my face. When he opened the door, we both looked at each other and knew this was a bad dream.

It was him. The one my gut told me it would be. He invited me in. I recognized him immediately when our eyes met. He was in town to work on his second novel. As we both attempted to find the appropriate words for this awkward moment, I found myself spewing more information than I needed. He knew me and I knew him. He was the one who got me the job with the company conducting publicity for him. He was, or so I thought, a friend. And now, I was the whore he'd agreed to pay for for the next hour.

I looked out the picturesque window, showcasing Manhattan's early evening beauty and said, "This is my first time."

I didn't stay more than five minutes. I exited as quickly as I had arrived. I searched frantically for a pay phone that worked. I finally found one on the subway platform as I waited to go home and hide from the world. I made the mandatory call to the agency as instructed and told the owner I couldn't do it. Boss man apologized and informed me he was on the other line with the writer. He was cursing him; not because the agency sent the wrong type, but because this man knew my mother. My mother had prepared a meal for him when he had visited Richmond and he felt it was a betrayal of her if he had violated her son. With his last apology and the promise to find something else for me, I hung up the phone as the subway approached. I vowed never to do that again. The next day as I attempted to figure out what to do with the bills, I received a call from a magazine that I had worked with to book interviews for my acts. They wanted me to freelance for them. I looked up and thanked God. He does work in mysterious ways.

೮ಂ೦ಜ

Soon as I had healed from the sudden departure of Thomas in my life, he walked right back in as if nothing had happened. His calls of checking on me turned into requests to see me. I was reluctant at first, but I missed him. I knew that he would find his way back to me. He knew how to woo me and capture my heart. He knew that I longed to make love to him for old time's sake. We were back together again. It was as if we had picked up where we'd left off. I still had questions about his true residency, but I didn't care, he was here with me. Everything was sweet again.

With the exception of work, I had begun to find my own voice. My boss had given me an opportunity to prove myself with a group that had mediocre success with a song featured on a motion picture soundtrack and serving as the opening act for a bubble-gum pop rapper. Since they had not released a single in a while, I had to focus on their history. Their management team was so impressed by my commitment to them, they eventually spoke to my boss about me serving as the group's tour manager. In this capacity, I would be able to travel with the group and ensure they made their press junkets, arrange press and serve as a cock blocker for the teenage girls who saw them as permanent meal tickets.

The trip was arranged for us to go to California for a week. It was my first time flying across country and I was a bit nervous at the prospects of spending six-plus hours in the air. I talked things over with Thomas and he thought it was a great idea. Since we were back together, we discussed what the future would look like for the two of us. We even revisited the conversation about being tested to make sure we were both negative, as we continued to have sex without a condom. I was encouraged to schedule the appointment and let him know the time and date and he would make sure he was there. I did as I was told, but he never showed.

Before I boarded the plane to California, I headed to the health department in Chelsea. The hanging posters reminded me of elementary school, colorful and with meaning. These posters, however, conveyed other messages that were forbidden in the elementary schools I had attended.

They called my number that was given to me and I was escorted into a private office by a kind, plump white woman. This was no different from the numerous times I had been tested before, but she offered more information to me than I had received in the past. She assessed my risk factors and explained the procedure to me. After this discussion, I was then led to another room, where my blood was drawn and I was instructed to call back within two weeks.

I left for California armed with a heavy itinerary for the group and a goal to have them appear on the then popular *Arsenio Hall* show. If I could pull that off, I was set in this trial run as tour manager. We spent the week doing press and other popular long-running television shows. I was having a great time with the guys, but I missed Thomas. We spent the night together before I headed to Los Angeles and he provided me with a lame-ass reason why he didn't show up to be tested. I accepted it as he held me in his arms that night. I figured when I received my test results and I was negative, there was no need for him to take the test.

It took me a while to get back into the swing of things when I returned from California. I found myself trying to catch up on as much sleep as possible, but it didn't help. I mustered up enough strength to get out of bed just to eat and on occasion take a shower. I had enough money to cover my bills from the freelance writing gigs and the recent week in Los Angeles, so I wasn't too pressed to return to the grind of a daily gig with the boss from hell. I knew other road trips were coming up for the group as they prepared for their new album release. I simply wanted to rest.

One night I was awakened from a deep sleep by a call from the health department. I had failed to contact them for my test results upon my return. I figured if anything were wrong, like my former physician in Richmond, they would have contacted me. I waited for them to give me the test results over the phone, and they informed me that they couldn't because of confidentiality issues. I arranged a date and time with them to get the results and left the message pad by my bed.

chapter thirteen

On December 6, 1993, I dragged my ass out of bed. I took a luke-warm shower, because the heat in the apartment was off again. I reached for a pair of baggy green-denim jeans I'd received from a clothing line represented by the company I worked for. I donned an emblazoned T-shirt of one of the groups I represented and grabbed the multi-colored flannel jacket Thomas had given me. I had to go into the office after getting my test results, so I grabbed the information I needed and stuffed it into my black suede backpack. My hair was still slightly damp, so I grabbed the baseball cap Kay had given me with her hip-hop committee's logo. Right before I headed out the door, I double-checked my wallet to make sure I had the card that was given to me a few weeks earlier with the assigned number "1277597."

As I rode the subway, I mentally planned the remainder of my day. I would get my test results and listen to the counselor instruct and encourage me to use condoms. I would take the literature once again and either discard it upon leaving, or just keep it in my office until I was tired of looking at it.

I bundled up tightly as the brisk air greeted me exiting the subway. I was ready for this to be over with. I wanted to put to rest the assumption that Thomas had about me being positive.

I entered the building at Twenty-eighth Street and Ninth Avenue and relaxed my jacket as I warmed up. I announced myself to the receptionist who asked to see my card, identifying me by the number "1277597." After confirming who I was based on this piece of paper, I sat down to wait for the young lady who would change my life forever.

She remembered me from our previous meeting. I had shared with her briefly my trip to California and my chance meeting with Arsenio Hall. I was able to secure an autographed photo for my mother who was a big fan of his. I had planned on giving it to her as one of her Christmas presents. I went on for a bit more and realized the time. I had things to do and I wanted to get this out of the way. I needed to go to the office and pick up my check and head to the grocery store. I was going to prepare a nice meal for Thomas and get all of his favorites. I also needed to get to the liquor store to pick up something for him and prepare for a nice loving evening.

She got up to retrieve the folder from the locked file cabinet that contained my test results. Once again, I was asked for the stub that contained the number 1277597 to confirm for her I was who I said I was. She opened the folder and placed it in front of me. She turned it so that the words "HIV Antibody Positive" faced me.

At 2:58 p.m. I attempted to swallow the uncontrollable sobbing. She reached over to me and rested her hand on my shoulder. I banged the back of my head against the wall behind me, crying hysterically. I couldn't stifle or silence myself from the others waiting in the lobby for similar news or actual good news. I found out that I was going to die.

Between the cries and seat fidgeting, hoping that this was all a bad dream, I managed to hear some of the clipped statements she had for me. I could tell from the tone and the rehearsed fashion, she had done this many times before and I was pretty sure there were many others who reacted the same way before me. She waited until I silenced myself for a moment to look at the paper again. She started to provide me with instructions on what to do next. For starters, I was told to quit smoking because the cigarettes contained toxins that were toxic to my immune system. She continued by telling me I needed to quit drinking, because it, too, was detrimental to my health. As if that wasn't enough, she stressed that I needed to peel my fruits and vegetables before I ate them, because they contained pesticides that were toxic to my compromised immune system. I sat there waiting for her to say, "Smile, you're on *Candid Camera*," but it never happened. After she handed me a list of resources and telephone numbers, she double-checked my mental status before she showed me the door.

I knew my way around the Chelsea area and how to get back to the subway to get to work, but I walked the longest walk to the entrance in a total daze. I tried not to cry because the tears became frozen quickly in the air. I did not want anyone to see me crying or notice my vulnerability. I boarded the train to work and watched my life pass me by with each passing stop.

Kay was on the telephone when I entered her new office. She had been recently promoted to director of publicity and her schedule was crazier than ever. She earned that title and was very deserving of it. She waved me in and instantly knew something was wrong. Whoever she was on the telephone with would have to wait. She informed them that someone was in her office and she would get back to them. Before I could tell her, I saw the sadness in her eyes as she looked at me and asked, "What's wrong?"

It hadn't been a full half hour before I found myself stumbling over the phrase I would have to use from this moment on: "I, I, am…" My voice trailed off as I sucked it in, delaying what I needed to say.

"Sweetie, what's wrong?" she searched again. Along with the words that came out, the waterworks started again. "I got HIV." On cue, she immediately came from around the marble desk that had been passed down to her by our boss and placed her arms around me. Since her promotion, she had served as a buffer between me and the diva sitting in the office next to her. She zipped my jacket up and sent me home. I tried to tell her I would be okay, I just needed her, and she hugged me again. She told me not to worry about work, to go home and take care of myself; she would handle any questions regarding my absence. She promised that she would call me later that evening to check on me once I got home. I admired her and had grown to love her as a sister. I wrapped myself up in her words and headed home. This didn't seam real. I rested my head against the nasty window of the A train, watching the lights disappear as the train sped up to Washington Heights. I played over and over the words the counselor had shared with me: "Don't drink, don't smoke." As I exited the train station, I stopped by the local liquor store two blocks from my house and placed my order: one fifth of Bacardi Dark and a pack of Newports.

I avoided the ice cubes from the freezer in the kitchen. I noticed through the slightly cracked door of my roommate's room, that he was home. I heard him as I grabbed a glass from the kitchen and closed my own bedroom door behind me. I wouldn't say he was an ideal roommate; this was more of a business arrangement and I was just a mere tenant. It had been a year and some change since I moved here and we barely said more than "hi" and "bye" to each other. Our communication consisted of notes left for one another on the table in the hallway. When it was time to pay my portion of the bills, he would leave the bill highlighted with the breakdown in charges. Had we developed a friendship, I could have easily barged into his room and cried on his shoulder, but I didn't.

I turned the light on next to my bed and before I even took my coat off, I poured myself the first of many drinks from the bottle of Bacardi. I searched for a CD to play, anything to prevent my roommate from hearing me cry. I had learned when Thomas was over, that he could hear our moans and groans through the wall. I found this out after Thomas and I had finished making love one night and noticed through that same crack in my room-mate's door as I headed toward the bathroom, that he was masturbating to the sounds coming from my room. I turned the volume up so that it wasn't disturbing, but just enough to cover and disguise my tears. I chased the taste of tears and snot with the rum that soothed me. I had all but forgotten about my planned evening with Thomas. I needed to see him as soon as possible. I needed him with me. I took another drink and prepared myself for the telephone call.

I was placed on hold for a brief moment until he picked up the receiver. He seemed agitated because they were short-staffed and he needed to fill in for one of the cashiers until someone came for their shift. My speech had begun to slur from the alcohol I had drunk and I started to cry again.

"What is it, what's wrong? I'm a little busy right now," he pushed out. I told him without hesitation the news I had just received. I needed to know if he was still coming to see me that evening. He paused for a moment and

I waited for some type of comfort, but it never came. Before he hung up the phone, he thanked me for the information and said he would call me back. That call never came.

I balled myself up in a fetal position aching not only from the news the counselor had given me, but also combined with the coldness in Thomas' voice. I cried myself to sleep listening to the CD that played continuously. I hadn't paid much attention to the lyrics of the Toni Braxton song before this evening, but as I closed my eyes, I heard the hurt in her voice. "I didn't have the strength to live, but much too young to die." I wiped my eyes, but the tears continued, burning as they flowed. I wanted so much to die at that moment.

My stomach was upset from not eating that day when I did finally wake up several hours later. I looked at the clock and saw that it read a little after midnight. I was still dressed and listening to Toni. By this time the Coke was room temperature, but cold enough to pour another drink. I reached for my backpack that contained the information and phone numbers of agencies to call if I felt I was going to do myself bodily harm. I looked at the flashing light on the answering machine and noticed there were a couple of missed calls. I rummaged through my bag as I pressed the "play" key to hear the messages. I listened to Kay's concern as she requested that I call her when I was ready to talk. The next message surprised me. It was my boss calling. He'd left the message that he had heard the news from Kay and wanted to see me the next day. He told me to hang in there and if I needed him, to call him, regardless of the hour. And that was it. I played the messages again, hoping that Thomas' message was sandwiched between the two, but it wasn't. I removed my jacket in which I had fallen asleep. It was now wrinkled from the position I stayed in to comfort me. I searched for the first number I could find to have someone to call to about what I was feeling. I contacted the first toll-free number on the list and dialed the numbers.

I took another swig from the drink while I waited to hear a human voice. Again I sucked back the tears and phlegm in my throat as I shared with the female voice on the other line the information I'd received. I said to her, when actually I was trying to convince myself, "I know I am not going to die."

Before I could finish my statement and request her help for assistance, she informed me that I was going to die. I broke down. I asked to speak to someone else on duty. I wanted to hear from someone else and not this insensitive bitch that I would be okay. I spent the next half hour with her supervisor. Her voice offered some hope. I felt through the telephone wires, her arms reaching out to me and holding me. No one else was going to do it. I stopped crying for a brief moment before I took off the remainder of my clothes to get into bed. I had all but killed the contents of the bottle, but there was enough for one or two more drinks. I pulled the covers up to my chest to warm me as the rum had. As I reached for the light to turn off, I decided against it. I figured if I did that, it would be the last light I would see.

I was surprised at the emotions my boss had shown me when I walked into his office. He'd hugged me and allowed me to cry. I couldn't find any more tears because I had used them all. We had sat down on his sofa facing each other and we talked. A lot of the conversation was a blur, but he'd shared stories of his friends living with HIV and how they were dealing with it. By the time I'd left his office, I'd gathered from the reception that everyone knew what was going on with me. If I needed anything, I could go to any of them. Before I'd left the office, my boss asked if I had told Thomas. When I gave him the run down of his response, he asked for Thomas' number. I went back home and stayed in bed for the next two days. I cashed my check before heading in and made another stop by the liquor store. I wanted to be well stocked for the next couple of days to refresh the tears I had lost.

I slept between the constant drinking over the next few days. I found moments to feed my appetite and settle my stomach. When I heard the knock on the bedroom door, I assumed it was my roommate asking for the rent. I had placed it in an envelope where we usually held our communication. I dragged myself out of bed. Thomas was standing there.

I cried as he walked toward me and held me in his arms. My tears were a combination of anger, sadness and joy. I was angry that he had waited so long to contact me after I had informed him of my test results. I was sad because I knew my diagnosis would change everything, and the joy came in just seeing him standing there. He came into the room and undressed. He crawled into bed next to me and I fell into a deep peaceful sleep, without a word spoken between us.

I was awakened by the humming coming from the television. I turned over to find Thomas still there. I rubbed the sleep from my eyes to see if he were a figment of my imagination. He turned the volume down and turned toward me. He stroked my face as he searched for the right words. When he spoke, I waited with baited breath to hear what he had to say.

He started by apologizing for not calling or coming to see me sooner. He did not know how to or even want to deal with my hysterics. I was numb from the news and the number of empty alcohol bottles that had now gathered at the foot of my bed. You son of a bitch. My hysterics? How else was I supposed to deal with this? I had just turned twenty-five and someone told me I was going to die. He continued, but his words got lost as they tried to make their way to my ears. I knew from that moment on that I had lost him. It was not his cross to bear. He asked if he could come see me later that night after he got off work, and if I still wanted him in my life. I don't know why, but I agreed to it.

He got dressed to head back home to change. From the smell, I knew I needed to find a shower quickly. I spent the next few minutes removing the last few days of bed sweat, lint and dried tears. I managed to eat something and changed the sheets before I got back in bed. I didn't want to face the world. I barely wanted to face the man in the mirror.

When he returned that night, I was sober for the first time in a couple of days. I wanted to have my wits about me when we discussed the next step in our relationship. Since he had sex on the regular, I knew from the time that we spent away from each other that I had not fucked or been fucked by anyone else—outside of the interview with the owner of the agency, and when that took place, we used a condom. My body no longer contained the smell of day-old perspiration. I was fresh and clean. He knew it and before we talked, he fucked me.

He pulled out a joint and handed it to me after we were finished. I thought about what had just happened and carried a load of guilt. I had read the information given to me and realized that I should no longer have sex without a rubber. But I didn't have the strength to tell the man I loved, the man that possibly infected me, that we needed to start.

When I discussed this with him, he shook his head. At that time, I didn't know for sure if he knew he was positive or if he was in denial. That information would come later. He turned his attention toward the television as I made the suggestion that he get tested. "Well, if you are positive, maybe I am too," was the only response I would get from him—until years later.

I couldn't fight with him. I was scared that each time he walked out the door that he would not return. But there were other fights I needed to face. It was close to the Christmas holidays and I was heading back to Richmond to spend time with my family. When I relocated to New York, I was a healthy 175 pounds, and now looking at myself in the mirror, it was very visible that something was wrong. When I did have the opportunity to weigh myself, the scale showed an emaciated 135 pounds. I needed to make some calls; I needed to pick up some weight.

On one of the many restless nights leading up to my trip to Richmond, I found myself still drinking anything that would numb the reality that I was HIV positive. I found myself lying on every angle of my bed in some fetal position, holding myself because there was no one else there to do so. I listened over and over again to Toni Braxton. "*I didn't have the strength to live, but much too young to die.*" I picked up the telephone.

The first call I made was to my cousin, the one who had told me when I came out to her some years earlier that she was disappointed. She urged me to call my mother immediately after I revealed the news to her. She felt most uncomfortable returning home for the holidays knowing that she had this information and was keeping it from the rest of the family. I promised her I would. She told me she loved me.

The next call awakened my mother. Her evening routine consisted of lying in bed and dozing off around the 8:30 hour. Here it was after midnight and I was sure that she was in a deep sleep. I heard her clear her throat before she said "hello" and with that one word, I started to cry.

Between the gasps for air and crying, I told her. It was the hardest thing

I have ever had to do. I expected to hear her cry as she did the night I told her I was bisexual. But she didn't. She demanded that I stop crying as only a mother could. At twenty-five, I obeyed her once again; I was my momma's boy. She reassured me that everything would be all right. She informed me my family was anxious to see me because it had been a year since I was last home. I was instructed to pack my things and get a good night's sleep. Before she ended the conversation, she told me she loved me and she couldn't wait to see me. "It's going to be okay, baby." For the first time since I'd heard the news about being positive, I knew she was right. She had never lied to me before, and she didn't lie to me that night.

chapter fourteen

When I arrived in Richmond that cold evening, I stood at my
mother's door. I was happy to be home, but I knew my arrival
brought bad news. I had prepared her beforehand but I knew
that things had changed. I rang the doorbell and she opened the door.
Before I could set foot in the house, her short arms reached out to me and
held me. This is what I needed, Momma's love and reassurance. She was a
short woman, but in her arms as she carried me in the house, I felt like a
child once again.

We spent the holidays not talking about HIV but talking about what to
do next. She wanted me home and she wanted me home soon. I really didn't
want to think about the idea of returning to Richmond because of Thomas.
I knew it was the best place for me to be, but I wanted to be with him. I
could tell by the looks from my family members as they gathered at my
mom's for Christmas they knew something was wrong. Just like every black
family I know, they decided not to address it. We just don't air dirty laundry
like that, at least not on a joyous occasion.

I promised my mother that I would think about coming back home and
let her know my decision after the first of the year; 1994 was just around
the corner and it was my New Year's resolve to spend the rest of my life
with Thomas.

෨෬

I knew that I was returning to a city that offered me nothing more than a death wish. I was no longer working full time for the public relations company and barely existing on freelance writing gigs I received from them. I commanded $300 per bio or press release I did for other companies and I received a small reimbursement for the articles I produced for the national hip-hop publication that sought me after my foray into the world of male prostitution. I was able to make ends come close together, rather than actually meet.

I assumed upon my return that Thomas and I would spend New Year's Eve together after a concert event I had to attend on behalf of the one remaining groups I worked with. But that was not to happen. I spent the evening ensuring that my group was on the bill of a prominent record label's schedule of performers that evening. The headline act for the evening's festivities was a new rap trio, featuring one of the most beautiful young black women I had the pleasure of meeting. We met in the green room of the concert venue and I found myself wrapped up in her spell. I spoke fondly of her career and the man in me came out. We spent the evening walking hand-in-hand after her performance, at times taking moments out of our walk to find a nice quiet place to sit and converse. A few members of the singing group I represented whispered their approval in my ear. They thought I was switching over and doing the "straight" thing. But, little did they know, I just wanted someone to be with for New Year's.

The New Year greeted me with Thomas' absence. I saw him maybe a day or two later and we fell back into the same routine. The smoking. The drinking. The fucking sans condom. It was as if he wanted to play Russian roulette. He still had not gone to the doctor for a test and we continued to have unprotected sex. I forced myself in my own way, to face my reality of a person living with HIV. I contacted a counselor to deal with the information and started the beginning of many medical appointments. Thomas accompanied me once to an appointment and it really hit me at that moment that I was positive.

When I alerted the receptionist about my appointment, she placed me in a reserved area where other persons living with HIV were seated. I didn't know much about the disease, but there was a chilling look on their faces. This was not the VIP section I was used to sitting in at concerts. This was an area of persons with compromised immune systems, the hospital staff wanted to avoid. I tried to fight back the tears as the EMT's brought a man in on a stretcher and placed him alongside our special section. No one wanted to handle him. Everyone was scared. I knew that at some point in my life, that would be me. I had always been what gay men called a "drama queen." In my thoughts, I would die this wonderfully tragic death, similar to that of Juanita Moore in the remake of *Imitation of Life*. A hush would be observed across the country in memory of my passing. I would be propped up in my casket for the entire world to see how such a beauty could be taken away. What I really faced was the inevitable lesions and continued weight loss. The sunken and sallow face that was once able to turn many heads. This was my somber reality.

I realized a couple of things after that first medical appointment. I realized that there was no future with Thomas and me. I saw him less and less and his calls were not as frequent. I also realized that I needed to go home. Whenever I looked into the mirror, I was constantly reminded of the bad decisions I had made in life. It was time to go back to Richmond and die.

I informed Thomas of my decision. There was nothing holding me in New York, no promise of love anymore. Who wanted to be with a fag who found out he had that gay man's disease? No one that I knew.

When he arrived that last night I was to see him, I had begun to distance my heart from him. Some would even say that I was cold. It was the only way I knew how to hide the hurt of leaving this man that I loved. We had a couple of drinks and puffed a little weed. We mutually agreed to have sex one last time. I closed the door behind him after we said our good-byes. I packed my bags and the few possessions I had acquired since living in New York and headed home to Richmond.

chapter fifteen

I moved home on a Saturday. My family gathered at my mother's house to welcome me back into the fold. I honestly thought they all came running to see how much time I actually had left. I could see how uncomfortable everyone was with my appearance. I was a pale fraction of the man who left less than two years ago to pursue a dream inside of him since his childhood. My clothing sagged off my body, as I found myself lifting my pants up to rest on what remained of my waist. I would catch out the corner of my eye, someone looking at me to see if it was okay to hug me or to hold me. I attempted to smile and assure them that I would be all right, but that didn't seem to help.

We sat in the den listening to music as my mother glided through the kitchen to cook up everything in the house to force me to eat. I had no appetite. Being here was bittersweet for me. It was great to lay my burdens down and actually rest. My first night back in my bed, I slept the longest and deepest rest I'd had in a long time. Now I was sitting here with my family, observing the sadness on their faces.

I watched my cousins' kids dance around and hug at my legs, happy to see me. Since I had become a master of disguise, I covered my thoughts, knowing that there was a possibility that I would not see them grow up. I got up to change the CD so that no one could read what I was thinking. As I opened the door to the stereo system, I felt these two tiny hands wrap themselves completely around my leg.

"My mommy cried for you the other night," my five-year-old cousin said as he looked up at me. I was puzzled by his sincere and honest revelation, which I am pretty sure he didn't understand. "She cried for you because she said you were going to get sick and die." My heart sank. He didn't realize what he had said to me, because shortly thereafter, he was chasing another little cousin around the house. I looked around and realized that these were the thoughts of everyone around me. For the next two years, I did die.

ഇന്ദ

I'd never really been religious. Every time I sought comfort or spiritual guidance in the church, the foundation of the black community, I felt ostracized because I loved men. I went as far as to have sex with a preacher with hopes that he could somehow save me. When we talked about the intimacy we shared and my own personal struggles with being gay and positive, he only told me to repent as he did each time after we had sex. I found him to be a hypocrite, so I found my own spirituality.

The few stories that I was familiar with from the Bible were loosely translated into made-for-television movies. I adapted from the story of Sampson and Delilah, the need to grow my hair long. Like Sampson, I felt it was the only source of strength I had. I figured if I allowed my hair to grow, I would be invincible. The next two years, I watched my hair reach the top of my shirt collar. I refused to cut it, much to my mother's disapproving looks. I had prepared my funeral. I knew that it was coming soon. I didn't work during that time because I didn't want to invest much into a job that I knew I would have to eventually leave. I didn't want to leave the house because I felt everyone around me could see this disease setting up camp in my body. Before I ventured out of the house, I had picked up the much needed weight I had lost, but I felt others could see that I was dying. No one saw it but me. I was paranoid. The only source of income I had was from my writing gigs for the magazine. It wasn't enough to sustain me, but it was something that I could do from home. I was ready for whatever happened. I was ready to be carried off to my final resting place.

Almost two years to the day I returned to Richmond, I woke up to the realization that I was not dead and that I was not going to die anytime soon. I looked at myself in the mirror and decided that it was time to start living. I called a friend who happily came by to cut my hair. He had complained that my hair was too long and I needed to let it go. It was time. I realized that my source of strength did not lie in my hair, but in my heart. My source of strength came from my mother, who told me the night I called her, "It's going to be all right." When he was finished, I removed the hair that had fallen and placed it in a bag as a reminder. Sometimes it is best to let go of something holding you down. When my mother walked in the door from work, she called out for me. I knew that she would be shocked at my new appearance, but she hugged me. "That's my boy."

chapter sixteen

To say that getting used to living with HIV was easy is a lie. It was difficult to hear at the age of twenty-five that you were going to die and to actually start preparing for it. That statement still haunts me. I found a doctor who told me otherwise. I started to learn how to live and deal with HIV versus allowing it to kill me. I got myself back in the workforce, with the assistance of a dear family friend and started to live again.

I didn't date, because I still found it difficult to tell anyone that I was positive. The only satisfaction that I had came in the form of masturbation to old porn films and the like. Sometimes, I would imagine someone with whom I was interested and that occasionally seemed to do the trick for me. I had no problems bringing myself to completion, but I was missing something. I was missing the tenderness that went along with the intimacy. I missed the gentle kisses, the body exploration; I missed feeling someone touch me. We never really miss it, until it slips out of our hands.

I knew staying in Richmond would place a cramp in my social life. It was a curse to be positive and have others know it, although, there were folks I knew to be positive as well. By this time, I started doing HIV/AIDS prevention work and was given the chance to move, yet again to Washington, D.C. I jumped at the opportunity. I figured a new environment and a new chance would afford me at least the smell, taste and touch of another body close to mine.

෧ඏ

I moved to Washington, D.C. in January 1997. I found a great little English basement apartment on Capitol Hill, only a few short blocks to work. I lucked up with the apartment and the landlords, who were a settled gay couple who took a chance on me, considering my bad credit. Once I received the diagnosis, I decided that I wouldn't pay any of my bills, since I was given such a short life expectancy. That was probably one of the dumbest decisions I made among many.

With the new job, I worked with high-risk youth in the Northern Virginia region. If you ask me, anybody who was fucking at the time was at risk. I met some of the most incredible young people in my life. For some, their lives had been touched by HIV personally, with the loss of family and friends; for others, they wanted to show the community service they were involved with on their college applications. Whatever their reasons, they each held and still hold a special place in my heart. Conducting outreach efforts with them on Saturdays kept me youthful. It allowed me to relive a childhood that I didn't have and simply laugh. That was something I rarely did.

In Washington, I realized that there was an HIV positive community, one that I elected not to be a part of. I conducted the work, I was living with it, but I didn't want to attend support groups or dating circles. It was still fresh in my thoughts after a couple of years. There were times in which I did find myself in situations where I would meet someone and if sex became an issue, I figured if I was using a condom, I didn't have to tell anyone. Those short dating cycles didn't last long, because I feared what would be said once I revealed my status after fucking.

I continued to go out with friends and flirt. That was one thing I was always good at doing. I could smile and hold someone's attention with my well-versed conversation. I remember one guy saying to me that he found me interesting because I had a way of allowing those around me to hold on to my every word. But little did these folks know, that I was probably one of the most insecure individuals they would ever meet. I wanted someone to tell me that I was handsome and I never heard it. I still got, "You are very pretty," and here I was a grown-ass man. I never acknowledged the comments with thank yous, because I remembered what my father had said to me many years earlier.

One night while out, I met a guy with the most alluring eyes. A black man with blue eyes and he didn't pay for them. He was a true redbone, almost clay-like. He had a sandy-brown mustache and goatee and he was bald. As I started to allow myself the opportunity of dating, I realized there was a certain type I was drawn to—light skin, bald and hairy. I was a sucker for a man with a hairy chest. After we exchanged numbers and our interests, a few days later we went on a date. Well, let me rephrase that, he came over to my house a few days later and sucked my dick. Before he left the next morning, he said that he came over with the expectation of doing it and would have been disappointed if he hadn't. Before he swallowed me, I did tell him I was positive. And before he finished, with my head in his mouth, he told me the same. His name was Ellis.

He was an older gentleman, forty-seven to be exact, but he had an incredible body for a man his age. He was spry and active, more so than I actually wanted in a partner. I had committed to giving this a go, since we were both positive and I assumed that we would do everything to protect each other. The fact that he told me he had syphilis when we started dating, should have indicated where the relationship would end up. I was sadly mistaken. I was always one who believed in monogamy. I thought once you found someone you liked and eventually loved, that there was no desire for anything or anybody outside of the world the two of you were creating. For him, his definition of monogamy was the two of us sleeping together alone and sometimes that didn't even happen. Because I thought I was in love, yet again, and he could not commit to being just with me, I consented to allowing him to explore his sexual desires, with me in tow.

By this time, Ellis had introduced me to the wonderful world of internet searching. I had used the World Wide Web at work for research and downloading information to assist me in my need for directions to and from locations for work. But outside of the standard use, I knew nothing about AOL and the additional uses it could provide.

I found out what screen names were for and how, based on a description and a scanned photograph, you could order sex and have it delivered in thirty minutes or less, of course based on your likes and dislikes.

I had become accustomed to doing recreational drugs with boyfriends in the past and this was no exception. We would smoke a joint, hop online and surf. My initial reaction to a threesome or group setting was that I could not do it, at least not with a boyfriend or a partner. I had several threesomes under my belt with single friends. But I wanted to make him happy. The first time, I lay there watching the man I said I loved and who in return told me he loved me, freely open his gaping asshole for another to fill. I felt nauseated at the sight, but this is what he wanted. And I wanted to please him.

After a while, I found myself turned off about the whole idea. The few times that Ellis and I were intimate by ourselves, turned out to lack the excitement of being with others. I'd never been one who thought his dick was anything to make some crawl the walls over, and after fucking him the first time, I knew that I couldn't fill his needs. Hell, he had been surgically stitched after taking one that was too big and this had happened a couple of times before he and I hooked up. So, I would sit there masturbating, he would lie there on his back, sometimes on his stomach with someone else in his ass.

Now some would find this disturbing and after a while I couldn't do it, but at least he was honest. Now that I reflect on it, we were consenting adults, but HIV/AIDS advocates around the country, around the world for that matter, would have had us drawn and quartered. The group thing to some is a bit out there, but the fact that we were both HIV positive, engaging in group sex with other HIV positive men and not using condoms, would have made many cringe. Hell, I knew better. But here were other HIV positive men I was having unsafe sex with, along with a man I loved who was positive. I truly had a death wish.

We found ourselves coming home from work to see what takers we had, who had left messages for an HIV positive duo. We even received invitations to bareback parties, which for me were out of the question, until he expressed interest in going. We did.

Right down the street from where the largest AIDS service organization in Washington, D.C. is located, there were monthly bareback parties for non-discriminating men. If you had a dick or a hole, you were allowed to attend. You would receive the invitation via e-mail and the instructions.

You would in return forward your expressed desire to attend with a photo, if you had one, and a description of yourself. You would receive a confirmation e-mail and date, time and location. After a certain time, the doors were locked and no other participants would be admitted.

We entered the dark building and made our way up the stairs. We paid the admission and were assigned a locker to store our clothing and any other items we brought. Off in the corner was a makeshift bar that consisted of a few bottles of alcohol, chasers and a bowl of snacks. I removed my clothing with the exception of my underwear. I looked around and noticed that the majority of attendees were middle-age white men ranging in all shapes and sizes. I searched for the bathroom so that I would be able to locate it in the event I found myself about to get sick. The door was open, preventing any privacy from the activities going on. There sitting on the toilet was a middle-aged gentleman stroking himself and serving as the receptacle for all recycled beer or liquids consumed by the patrons. I stood there in amazement as I looked around to see things I had only seen in adult films. Off to my left, on a mattress placed in the middle of the floor, was a guy with both his ass and mouth being filled. I could tell that the guy who was behind him had reached his moment. The one in the front removed his dick from his mouth and proceeded to rim what was left behind by the other. Once he lapped and drank what was inside, he inserted himself. Within moments, he repeated the same display, removing his juices from the same guy.

I stood there and watched, somewhat intrigued by the freedom, somewhat sickened by what was going on. By this time, Ellis had removed every stitch of his clothing. He waited impatiently by me. I assumed, based on our conversation, that we were only there as observers. He had another agenda that had changed from the time we exited his car.

He spent all of five minutes beside me, before he excused himself to walk around. Before he could go any farther than fifteen feet in front of me, he was on his knees sucking off a group of four guys that had caught his eye. He serviced each one. Upon completion, I watched him disappear to a room on my right. I stood and pushed hands away that searched for my crotch. Now don't get me wrong, my dick was hard, but I knew that I was there to watch.

I waited for him to return. Five minutes passed. Ten minutes passed. I was nervous to make my way into the much darker room where he had headed, but I needed to see what was going on. I slowly found my footing and headed in the same direction. This was, as they say, the hub of the action.

On mattresses thrown on the floor and tables used to make makeshift beds that were already taken, I watched as white legs were raised around brown shoulders. Heads were thrown back to accommodate men who were holding the legs of these bottoms for deeper penetration. On the floor I viewed dark bodies bent over in doggy-style positions, sandwiched between white men, while another was underneath taking these brothers in their mouths. The moans and smell were overpowering. Not the smell of un-cleaned asses, but unbridled sex. I walked further into the den, searching for Ellis; I wanted to get him so that we could leave. I had a raging hard-on, but I couldn't bring myself to do anything in such a large and open setting.

I walked slowly, so that I wouldn't trip over anyone or interfere with the throes of passion. At the end of this room, I entered another area where the light showed me enough of what was going on. There I watched my boy-friend re-create for another group of four, his years of perfected oral skills. They stood around him, the thin-framed white boys, looking down on this brother. While he had one in his mouth, he grabbed on for two more. He made sure that each one had a turn in his mouth. He stood up, keeping the bigger one in his mouth and bent himself at the waist. At that moment, one of the individuals he had lubed with his saliva entered him with very little resistance. He balanced himself as they played back and forth in him and on him. By the time he had finished, everyone in the circle had taken a ride.

He stood up to give the bigger one he had accommodated in his mouth a go at his stretched hole. As he started to do this, he saw me staring at him. He immediately shook his head at the guy and I could read his lips, "No, not right now." He jumped off and headed toward me. I turned to see him head in my direction. He followed me to the locker as I got dressed. I couldn't stomach this anymore. I had had enough and from watching him, so had he. He was pissed with me as we got in the car. I had interrupted his play, but I couldn't watch anymore.

We didn't talk for a few days. When we returned to his apartment, I went home. I don't know whether he returned to the party, but I could tell he was still hot in the ass for more. I couldn't and wouldn't oblige. When we finally saw each other a few days later, he told me he loved me and he would try to control his urges. That didn't last long.

I was so fucking stupid. I knew walking into this was what I was getting. I felt like I didn't deserve better. We were both damaged goods. But I wanted someone in my life. After hearing his promise of controlling his libido, I allowed him to move in.

He hadn't been there a good solid two weeks before it started all over again. During this time, I had started to explore the internet on my own. I had created my own screen name and had developed my own group of friends. After watching him give himself so freely, I couldn't imagine what I could do for him other than provide the venue and the setting for his performances.

On the rare occasions that I was able to roam the internet myself, I started chatting with one guy in particular. He traveled a lot for work and after Ellis saw his pictures, he definitely wanted to hook up with him. I always avoided the possibility of the three of us getting together because my chat buddy seemed so pure and innocent. I didn't want him to be yet another notch on the metal bed post that Ellis and I shared. He was mine. His name was Jason.

Ellis and I only lasted a month longer after he moved in. I had lost count of the number of men we fucked, sucked and entertained in that basement apartment. At last count there were about eighteen that we both played with. Actually we had sex more with others than we did with each other. Before he moved out, he informed me that he had sex with both of my landlords while I wasn't home. How true that was, I don't know, but if it happened, it serves me right.

During this breakup, I continued to chat daily with my online buddy. I looked forward to seeing him pop up online. He helped me make it through this adjustment of being alone all over again. He traveled so much for work, that when he was in town, I was not and when I was, he wasn't. We spent hours online, catching each other up on our lives. We both agreed that at some point we would have to meet. Hell, I was used to getting out of one bad relationship and going into another. It was all I knew and ours would be just another in a line of them.

ഇൻ

I had planned to have my date with Jason early in the evening; that way if he looked nothing like the photographs that he'd sent me, I could easily use the excuse that had been used on me several times before: "I have to get up early."

It was a beautiful August evening, so I had the windows of my basement apartment open to capture the remaining daylight. I kept the door open with the gate locked so that I could actually see him before I opened the door to determine whether the date would last longer than an hour. I didn't understand why I was being picky. In the past month, I had allowed men I wouldn't usually give the time of day, the pleasure of lying in my bed and in my boyfriend's ass. So when had I decided to come up with a case of morals at that point?

I heard the doorbell ring while I was in the kitchen. I waited a moment, not to seem too anxious. I shook my head a time or two to stall for time and headed toward the gate. He was taller than I'd imagined, as he ducked his head to avoid hitting the edge of my landlord's porch. I allowed him entry into my own small enclosed porch as I unlocked the gate and opened the front door.

I sized him up from the time I saw his eyes. For some reason, the white boys that I had encountered had never really met an iron before, outside of their casual dress clothes for work. His jeans were slightly wrinkled, as if he had pulled them from the laundry basket just for this occasion. He wore a multi-colored striped shirt, reminiscent of Linus of the famed "Peanuts" cartoon. Since it was the summer, he had elected to frost his hair with blond highlights that had grown out, exposing his deep-brown natural roots. But he was cute.

I had learned from past dating experiences to allow the volume of the television or radio to appear slightly louder than usual. If the conversation that I was being pulled in to bored me, I could easily shift my attention from the mundane to the summer repeats. But it didn't matter with Jason. His eyes sparkled. Our conversation flowed as if we were still online, with many miles between us and only our fingers to tap and speak for us.

We lost the daylight as nightfall greeted us. I knew that I had to go out of town within the next day or two and there were things I needed to take care of, but Jason stayed that night. We both had expectations of a little something-something and that's what I got. When I showed him the door the next morning, we agreed to see each other upon my return. Here we go again.

Jason was an interesting character. I had come out in my life and work environment, but maintained some sense of "manliness" to keep my family, especially my father, at bay. For Jason, you could hear him from the other side of the country when he kicked open the doors to come out. My father had only seen the images of gay men and women on television, so he only saw us the way the media portrayed us, as screaming queens, sashaying up and down the streets, crying for our rights. I knew that if I was to ever take Jason to meet my father, I would have to deal with the I-told-you-so looks. I needed to prove my father wrong, but not in this case; I would keep a safe distance between the two.

I had tried mending the relationship with my father over the last couple of years. He was not too happy when I informed him of my HIV status. When I found the nerve, he responded as he always did without thinking, "I figured this would happen because of your lifestyle. I tried telling you this when you told me you were that way."

For almost two years I avoided him. I refused to answer the phone when his number appeared on the caller ID. I could hear my mother cursing him. "Why don't you fucking call him to find out how he is doing?" She was tired of being caught in the middle. I had done a great job of avoiding my father and his numerous questions until he sidelined me one day and showed up.

We tried to find even ground to talk. It was difficult at times within the few minutes he spent with me that day. I really didn't want him in my life after turning his back on me. I'd had enough. I was grown now and I didn't need his approval, but I still longed for his acceptance.

When my father arrived to visit me, I reluctantly sat down with him. My mother walked away to give us some privacy. Within a few minutes, he had already searched for the jugular and severed it once again. "So how's that thing going that you got?"

I didn't quite understand the question because it caught me off guard. "What thing?" I fished.

"You know that thing you caught?" And then it clicked. My father couldn't bring himself to say "HIV," just "that thing."

I sensed that there really was no sincerity behind the question, so I sarcastically responded, "Well, it's there, it's doing its thing." Before the conversation could go any further and play out the way it had in the past with me feeling inadequate, a friend showed up at the door to save me.

෨෬

Jason and I were going strong. We spent weekends and some weeknights together before we had to part ways for other parts of the country for days on end. When we were together, we made up for lost time. We both entered the relationship with the agreement that we would not use condoms. What was the use? We were both positive and there really was no fear of infecting each other. But every day at work, I was reminded by articles discussing re-infection, super infection, drug resistance, but I did not want to stop having unprotected sex with him. What made matters worse; we were both on the same drug cocktail. In the mornings, he would lay my meds out next to a glass of orange juice, facing his same two pills and his glass. We would swallow them at the same time as we did each other the previous night. He was in the medical field and reassured me that he had done his research and we were at minimal risk for drug resistance. We both knew better, but we continued.

As I had done in the past, I wanted to secure this relationship. I really wanted this one to last. I thought, as I had before, that this was someone I could spend the rest of my life with. I found myself spending more and more time at Jason's, eventually just paying rent for an apartment that I only visited to pick up my mail. Eventually, after a short time I moved in with him. Can we say "crash and burn"?

The first few weeks of co-habitation were great. We spent time redecorating and making room for my things. Although I had free reign of the place, it never quite felt like home. I felt more like the houseboy than the boyfriend/partner. Ass was given to me freely and abundantly for doing the simplest of chores. Emptying the trash, I would get a blowjob. Vacuuming, he would swallow. Dusting and doing the windows, full-out deep dicking. As I got better and better at the daily household chores, I was rewarded with other interesting uses for my body parts.

There were things I was used to doing as a sexual being. I enjoyed mutual oral gratification. Finding the right position to give pleasure and receive pleasure was always fun. I found lying on my side didn't work. I wasn't a lazy lover, but I loved someone atop me when providing oral pleasure, that way I could allow my fingers to run along the crack of their ass, searching. I loved fucking. I loved feeling my juice freely flow without a condom deep in Jason's ass. I could feel his muscles tighten, his long fingers digging into my ass to invite me deeper into him.

When he wanted to demonstrate his skills as a top, I allowed him entry into me. Before this could happen, I requested that he remove the Prince Albert jewelry that adorned the head of his dick to prevent any damage to my insides. I was not about to have my insides ripped out or the jewelry coming loose and getting lodged in my ass. I would even go as far as allowing my tongue to taste and pleasure the puckered hole I drilled daily. I made sure that I was there each and every time when Jason cleaned. I was not one into tasting mud or shit, if you know what I mean. And that was it.

I learned while living with Jason that he had a few fetishes. Hell, I think we all do. For me, there is nothing sexier than seeing a man in a nice pair of form-fitting boxers, teasing you with the surprise. But that was it for me. Jason, on the other hand, had other ideas.

We showered in preparation for a night of passionate sex. We started out with a couple bottles of wine to set the mood. We never smoked rolled joints; we always used one of the many water pipes he had acquired during his travels. The music drifted throughout the condo at a low hum. When it was time to adjourn in the bedroom, a CD was placed in the player at a low volume and the huge candles were lit. We met in the middle of the bed to begin.

I loved kissing him as I did all the others. He tasted sweet from the wine and if the mood hit me, I would allow the Prince Albert to tickle the back of my throat before I felt myself about to gag. When deep throating was required, I had learned how to loosen the ring with my tongue so that I could remove it. A brotha had skills.

Our petting was intense, every now and then knocking the cat or two off the bed as we went from corner to corner. One night as we took a break, I watched as Jason disappeared into his closet.

When he returned, he had something wrapped in a number of towels. I never went into his closet, other than to hang something up. I was instructed not to go searching for anything and I obeyed his wishes. He placed the wrapped package on the bed and revealed its contents.

Now, I was no virgin. I had seen sex toys before, but none like this. In all shapes, sizes and colors were an assortment of dildos. Some with dual heads, some with extended ticklers, ribbed edges and balls increasing in size attached by a mere cord. I thought to myself, *That shit is going nowhere near me.* But it wasn't for me.

Jason wanted to introduce me to the art of ass play. He lay on his back, with his legs equal distance, slightly bent at the knees. He reached for the elbow lubricant we used for penetration and applied a heaping on the mid-sized dildo. We were used to the poppers and he grabbed the bottle that was next to him on the nightstand. He inhaled. I watched carefully as he lubed the dildo as he would usually lube me for entry. He raised his knees, bringing them closer to his chest. He placed the head of this object at the entrance I wanted to be in. He used his fingers to guide it in and he closed his eyes. While the one hand worked the tool in and out, he reached for my hand. He placed it on top of the dildo and provided me with direction. He asked that I go slowly at first. I felt the hard plastic disappear deep inside him. He had no use for it after a while; he was ready to move on.

I used the various plugs and balls on him until I felt myself drip. He was so loose that if I ventured to guess, I could take a flashlight and see clear up to his throat. He whispered that he wanted me inside of him. I was happy to replace the plugs with my throbbing hard-on, but that was not what he wanted.

He grabbed my hand, placed it at his loose opening and slid in my fingers. With the two fingers inside, I could feel that I could freely move them around in a circular motion. He wanted more. I inserted another finger, but that wasn't enough. He reached for my hand and applied the elbow grease to it. He took another hit of the poppers and guided my hand deep into him.

A euphoric feeling rushed over me as I now knew that I was up to my wrist in Jason. I closed my eyes as I felt the moisture and warmth engulf my hands. I was frightened a little because I didn't want to hurt him, but I had no control over the situation. He was driving. I took his lead and applied additional lubricant to my arm. He lowered himself further onto my arm. As he did with the toys, he rode my wrist. I wanted to bust, but it felt too good. We continued with this for a while, until he released my wrist. He reached for me, legs in the air, his hands resting on the back of his thighs and guided me inside him. When it was over, I collapsed on top of him and thanked him for my lesson.

Our daily fucking was now replaced with fisting. Jason couldn't get enough and I wasn't getting enough.

There were times during the relationship that we were just not fucking. He only wanted to be held. He tossed and turned some nights from bad dreams, awakening to cold sweats and frightened memories. I would comfort him and ask if everything was okay, but he just wrapped my arms around him and refused to share. When he did share, it was with the assistance of the ounce of pot he purchased once a month from his dealer. Not only did we smoke it, we ate it. He baked it in brownies for dessert. We would sit stoned out of our heads, me hoping for some sex, him braving the information he would share.

Once Jason felt comfortable from the THC, he would sing, not songs on the radio, but sad songs of his life. He would cry as he told me of the abuse he encountered from his father. He never exactly stated what type of abuse, but I could tell it was traumatic. He shared his stories of abandonment, when his parents left him in a cabin in Minnesota during brutal winters when they went off for work. He was left with a supply of food and the bare essentials to survive. My heart reached out to him and held him. He cried and I shared in his tears.

One story that haunted me was his story of sexual abuse. It wasn't his story of surviving the abuse, but his role in portraying the abuser. He had sexually molested his cousin who was a few years younger than him at the time.

The story itself didn't come to the forefront of my thoughts until Jason and I visited my family over the Christmas holidays. Everyone had met him before and had taken a liking to him. But I noticed his interaction with my little female cousins. I quickly reprimanded them and demanded that they go into the other room to play. I don't think Jason suspected that there was a fear that I could not convey to him or to my family. I never shared it with my family. I thank God that my family members did not fall victim to his deviant behavior.

But it wasn't only this lingering thought of him molesting his cousin. It was his desire for me to abuse him in ways I couldn't imagine. He had rape and bondage fantasies that turned him on that I couldn't get into. Upon my return from a trip to Kentucky and checking e-mails before returning to work, there were a number of rape websites visited during my absence, with screen names and profiles of bondage masters. I couldn't do this anymore. The innocence that initially attracted me to him had now been replaced with someone I no longer recognized. The night I returned saw the end of Jason and me.

I so had wanted this one to work. Maybe for all the wrong reasons, again of wanting someone in my life—to validate me. I went so far as to propose marriage to Jason. After returning from another trip away from each other, I purchased a ring, symbolizing our love. Made in the form of what appeared to be bricks, it created and laid the foundation for what I assumed we both wanted. I was nervous as I knelt there asking him to share his life with me. I wanted it to be the one—the lasting one.

After attempting to reach him numerous times while I was in Kentucky, fears of his betrayal interrupted my thoughts. The reviews I received from the participants of the leadership workshop I taught that weekend, clearly showed me that my focus on work was not there, but more so on Jason and what he was doing.

When he picked me up from the airport, he couldn't answer about his absence when I'd tried to reach him during my trip. My anger started to simmer. It was continued with the help of the six-pack of beer I picked up en route home and continued when I saw what he had been doing online while I was away. I was hurt. I was devastated. I was fucking angry. I had once again invested my time and my love into a relationship that was going nowhere. I needed to express my anger. And as I left the home that we shared that evening for good, I made it a point to hurt him as much as he had hurt me.

Hell hath no fury like a gay man scorned. I found creative ways to get even with the man I said I loved, but it all turned out to show that there was nothing but contempt and hatred for him. Because of my actions, he never spoke to me again. I can understand why.

I still see him online from time to time. I try to say hello, but he never responds. I hope he has found what he is looking for, because I couldn't give it to him.

മോങ്ങ

I threw myself back into work. I lucked up at the recommendation of a co-worker and found a place deep into Alexandria, Virginia, a suburb of Washington, D.C. I thought it was far enough for me to stay out of trouble yet close enough to endure an hour commute to work. My sexual gratification came from fucking individuals while I was out of town for work. No strings, no-frills sex. I found myself drinking more and more on those lonely nights I lay in my empty bed in my empty apartment.

Once I got my internet connection going in my new place, I was online every night seeking companionship. It amazes me how far someone will travel just to get a nut. I had nasty bottoms from Washington, D.C. who wanted to be fisted and who would journey in the middle of the night to Route 1 for the comfort of my fist. Even closer, I found conquests that would come over to suck my dick. One night, with a raging hard-on, I had to piss. Before I could excuse myself, he granted me permission to let the waters flow. He didn't spill a drop.

∞⦰

Shortly after I had exhausted the use of the internet, I was bored. I wanted more. The alcohol didn't do it for me and the revolving door of sex partners only satisfied my release. Sometimes I would host group settings as I did with Ellis just to have someone there. The more men there, the longer they would have to stay, in order to pass themselves around among the crowd.

My co-worker expressed her concerns for me. Rightfully so, I was out of control and I didn't know how to reel it back in. I fell into yet another relationship, where jealousy reared its ugly head and once again, I was acting out. I was a man on the edge.

I eventually lost my footing when family, friends, loved ones and fuck buddies felt me spiraling out of control. I lost my job, I lost loved ones, but the most important thing I lost was me. My mother's love couldn't help me this time.

I was given no choice in this situation. I needed to run and run quickly. I needed to go somewhere where no one knew me and start over. I needed a fresh start. I needed to step away from everything and everybody in order to find me. I was a lost soul waiting to fly off the cliff and that time was coming soon. No matter what the HIV was doing, I was spiraling out of control. I made a few calls and contacts and a month after leaving Washington, D.C., I found myself in New Mexico.

ഇൻരു

I boarded the Southwest flight out of Baltimore-Washington International Airport ready for a new change. I needed to reinvent myself and discover the true essence of me. Until 2002, I had done everything for everybody and left myself out there with nothing. I accepted a position with an AIDS service organization in Albuquerque, with my reputation still intact and questions running through the heads of friends and associates about this choice I made. They figured that it was only part of who I was. They had gotten used to my antics. I needed to try again. I needed to find my way back into their hearts.

After we descended, I searched the curbside parking for my associate Mike. After two weeks with him, I had purchased a new car and found a nice two-bedroom apartment. It was sparsely furnished. I didn't want to invest the time in staying here. I would only put in enough time to regroup and work things out. I'd had it with the East Coast and I ran away to try and find myself.

The adjustment initially was difficult. Albuquerque only had a small African-American population, approximately three percent. It took me almost three months to actually find a place where I could get a haircut, some conversation, and some sense of family at the local black barbershop.

I became a popular case manager on staff. For all newly diagnosed individuals who enrolled in services, a great deal were assigned to me. I was the only staff member of thirty-three who was living with HIV, so to show the success of living with this dreaded disease, I was assigned those clients who were on the edge, very much like me.

Each case manager also was assigned other duties outside of the standard services provided daily. I was approached to facilitate a discussion group for HIV positive men in the community. The agency really didn't have high hopes for the group; they wanted to burn off some funding and show that they at least created something, even if the community did not support it. I wanted this group to be different from the others that had not been successful in the past. I wanted the group to reflect the needs of the community. I set about the task of developing it and created the first flyer.

We had our first meeting on a Tuesday night. A total of eleven participants showed. I found that disconcerting, since we provided services to approximately six hundred people in the community. Of course we discussed the focus of the group, recruitment and retention efforts and possible topics. I reinforced that I was there to facilitate the discussion and provide correct information. If anything, it was more like sitting around at someone's house breaking bread. Within a matter of weeks, the group grew by leaps and bounds. Seating was very limited and the desire to share feelings and emotions in a safe place, without judgment, had been created.

Word had spread throughout the city about this new black case manager and his commitment to the HIV positive community. I later heard that some of the guys only came to the group to check me out to see if I was fuckable. I was a new face, in a new place and possessed a reputation with flair.

I managed to maintain the integrity of my role for a period of time. It was difficult to establish my own identity outside of work. Everywhere I went, I was associated with my role as case manager at the agency. I found it difficult to go to a bar, without running into at least half the clientele we served. There were lines that could not be crossed. But of course, I would find a way to erase them.

ℰℭ

He walked into the group with an air of sensuality floating around him. I am a stickler for details and remember sizing him up. He wore a pair of black jeans that showcased the bulge on the right side of his leg. He opted not to wear underwear in order to show off his goods. He sported a black fringe jacket, reminiscent of the late 1980s, and a black cap. During the conversation that evening with the other group members, I caught myself stealing looks at him and impressed that he paid attention to what each person shared. His name was Samuel.

He stayed behind along with some of the other regulars, to thank me for the work that I was doing. He helped rearrange the room for the following day's meeting and smiled as he said good night. I was certain that he was not young, based on the smile lines that showed right next to his eyes, but he was special. He found a way to contact me on occasion to share with me his ideas for the group and suggestions to improve attendance. He was as concerned about promoting empowerment as I was, but whenever he singled me out to talk one-on-one, I found myself avoiding this direct contact. I didn't want to appear to show favoritism to one member of the group, but sometimes I couldn't help it.

At times I felt like I needed a boost from the staff and management to assure me that I was doing a good job with the group. My supervisors received letters from the participants thanking the agency for creating this new and exciting discussion group, not a support group. There were other groups that provided support.

Samuel encouraged others in the group to share with the management of the agency how their lives had been transformed as a result of these bi-weekly gatherings. He went as far as to take pen to paper and put into his words what he got out of the group.

I felt this attraction to him that grew stronger each time we saw each other and a desire to want to be with him. I threw caution to the wind and made up some lame-ass excuse to meet him for coffee to discuss the group. I struggled with this attraction toward Samuel. I knew that other staff members had dated clients of the agency, if they didn't provide any direct service to the client.

Samuel provided me directions to his house for coffee. I had my own agenda. It had been a while since I had been laid. I really needed to get off and he was the one who lit the fire for me.

I entered his home and was amazed that someone on disability could afford such a place. His home was newly built in an affluent community. He greeted me with a pleasant hug and made his way to the open kitchen to retrieve two cups of coffee.

We spent the afternoon talking about each other. I made sure that I would not allow him to see the cracks in my foundation that had led me to this place. No one knew of my previous existence, other than I was from the East Coast. We spent the afternoon laughing and sharing stories of living with HIV. We decided in the early afternoon to switch from coffee to tequila and headed to the grocery store for a bottle of Cuervo.

We returned and discussed more topics, including movies, music and television. He had an incredible collection of films I had not seen and he was kind enough to introduce me to some of his favorites. We enjoyed shots of Cuervo between the tears of beautiful love stories that made us both cry on cue, and side-splitting humor of cancelled comedies.

I knew that I was unable to drive at that moment and didn't want to risk getting a ticket or encountering an oncoming motorist in getting back home. We were both drunk from the tequila and he asked if I wanted to rest for a moment. We made our way to his ground-level bedroom.

He removed his clothing, exposing the package that had caught my eye the first night that I saw him. I couldn't control the stiffening in my pants at the time; I removed mine to lie next to him. I felt his hands reach for my crotch, as he leaned to kiss me. The bedroom was dark and possessed a certain coolness that my apartment could not generate. Being from the East Coast, I was used to central air conditioning and the majority of the homes here only provided swamp coolers. As he straddled me, grabbing his small-ass cheeks, he mounted me until I came. We fell asleep shortly thereafter.

When I saw Samuel at the next group meeting, I felt a tinge of guilt, trying not to single him out. I had hoped that the other members would not find out or discover that I was fucking him every chance I could get. Sometimes I slipped away during my lunch hour for a quickie with him. He would greet me at his front door in a jock strap, bent over, and because of timing, I quickly released myself. I could have waited until the group ended some months later, but I loved the sex I was getting. I loved the way he would look up at me after bringing me to completion, his eyes searching for my approval to tell him thanks. I was never dissatisfied.

I continued my pattern with Samuel as I had with Thomas and Jason. We were very discreet with each other in public but totally sexual beings behind the gated community. He asked if I wanted to move in, and because my lease was up, I agreed. It wasn't that I needed a new place, but I figured if he was sucking and swallowing me, who else was he doing it to? By moving in with him, it allowed me to make sure that I was the only one in his life and in his bed. It was an opportunity to make sure that he wasn't cheating on me.

I couldn't help but think he was like the others. Hell, everybody else had cheated and he was no different. He was a man, right? The same way that he decided to attend the group, as he later confessed to find new sex partners, I figured with him being home all day, any unsuspecting cable guy, window washer or grounds man benefited from his willingness to please.

Samuel shared stories with me of his sexual appetite. I sometimes used these stories to get me off when I found my dick difficult to perform after inhaling too much of the poppers. I would listen as he shared with me stories of big dicks taking total control of his thin and wiry frame. There was something about the abuse of his hole that turned me on; taking me to the point I needed and wanted to get. I felt guilty afterward and the thoughts of him cheating continued to consume me. I know it sounds twisted, but it was all I knew.

We continued this course of drinking and fucking and sucking after I moved in. We even invited one or two others to join us.

The few guys we played with were white and he wanted another black man to dominate him as well. We found some guy from a distant city in New Mexico who came to visit. We prepared for the evening. He was in the shower using the sure shot to clean himself thoroughly, and I was on the sofa building up the courage with tequila.

When we did play with one of the regular white guys, we sat around and talked before anything happened. They were friends and there was some sort of connection. When the brother entered, Samuel immediately fell to his knees and began to tease him with his mouth.

I watched as he savored the taste of this man, excluding me; it was as if I wasn't there. My jealousy began to boil over. We adjourned to the bedroom, where he wanted me to take him first. In sizing myself up next to this man, I knew there was only so much I could do. I whispered in Samuel's ear after I came, that I didn't want this to happen. I had made a mistake. I didn't want this man to fuck him. That was not my decision to make.

I told him he needed to tell him to go. I walked out of the house and headed to my car to clear my head. What the fuck had I done? I was going off, leaving my partner in our bed with another man. I quickly returned.

When I entered the house after clearing my head, I was hoping to see this guy about to exit. There was no one in the living room. I noticed that the back door was open, but there was no sign that they were out there.

I heard Samuel's moans coming from our bedroom. I bolted into the room to see him on all fours getting fucked. I freaked out. I demanded that this man leave immediately. Don't say a fucking word, get out.

When he left, I flew into a rage. How could he do this to me? I told him I didn't want this to happen. He disobeyed me. I only saw red. You son of a bitch.

I tried to choke the living life out of him. I saw his eyes roll back but I didn't care. He'd hurt me. He managed to get away and stand up. I stumbled from the three-fourths bottle of tequila I had drunk, but my fist connected with the side of his face as I punched him. He cried as he begged me to stop, but I wasn't in control. He got away and ran to the bedroom upstairs as I tried to break the door down. I caught myself. I was having flashbacks of past hurts and I was taking everything out on him. I retreated to our bedroom and wept.

I watched as Samuel tiptoed around me the next day. He feared that I would hurt him again. I was so apologetic for my actions and he accepted them by accepting me. In a roundabout way, he did inform me it was my fault and I knew that.

I couldn't control this rage burning inside me. I had convinced him to do this deed for me, only to back out at the last minute. It took a day or two for him to regain the hearing in his ear from the blunt force of my fist. I was sorry for my actions, but I couldn't help feeling betrayed. I needed to strike back. I needed to do to him what he had done to me. My revenge came in the form of his brother.

Bob and I had made eye contact with each other when we were introduced by Samuel. There was an interest on my part, but I wouldn't go there because of my relationship with Samuel. This time I did.

I should have invested in stock in Cuervo, as much as I consumed it. I continued to throw up the fact that Samuel had hurt me. I sucked back the tequila as I maneuvered the twists and turns of the winding road leading to Bob's house.

He greeted me at the door with nothing on. He had not expected company. He was used to sleeping in the nude, from what he'd told me. We didn't speak a word as I followed him into Samuel's old bedroom we slept in when we visited. I fucked him as I had fucked Samuel in the same bed. I rinsed my dick off in the sink and without a word of good-bye, headed back home to Samuel.

He wasn't in a deep sleep as I whispered in his ear, "I just fucked your brother." I heard the tears hit the pillow, but found some demented pleasure in telling him about it.

During the rest of my days with him I apologized. He accepted the apology when I first made it, but for me that wasn't enough. We both knew that it was time for us to move on. Too much hurt had taken place—on both parts. As with all of my exes, we had sex one last time before I made my way back home. I still saw him standing in the driveway as I pulled out. I refused to look back in the mirror because there was no turning back. One more down, many more to go.

chapter seventeen

It took me three and a half days to make it back to Richmond. I watched the barren land of the Midwest turn green and vibrant as I approached home. In the two short years I had been gone, much had changed about the city I called home. The landmarks I visited on the main street running the length of the city were now gone. The city was going through an overhaul. The bridge that connected the north and south side of Richmond was barely hanging on from its demolition. I was coming home yet again. The one place I always ran to when I had fucked up.

I had been home a few months before I landed a job at a local university doing, what of course, more HIV/AIDS work. When I visited the bars that molded me, I saw the same friends I had known from the early days. Nothing had really changed, but the names of the locations. Every Friday night, the men of color congregated at the front of the club, taking up the few booths that occupied the entrance. Once in a while, you would see a few black men intermingle with the Caucasian crowd, because of their desires for them. Me, I was an equal opportunity fuck. I liked them all, sometimes I liked them together. I hated coming back to this place and the same rat race. Before landing the job, I started to really push my body to the limit with alcohol. It didn't matter what type, just as long as it soothed me. I resorted to the internet once again for quick fixes for my sexual needs, never really developing any long-lasting relationships. It was cyclical.

I slowed my roll when I entered the university. I elected to limit my drinking to the weekends; during the week that honor was held by one of my fellow staff members. It was obvious from his glazed-over look, that hiding in his desk drawer was something to take the edge off. At times my fellow co-workers and I had to back away from him when he addressed us because you could smell the alcohol seeping out of his pores. He was nothing more than a functioning alcoholic. I worked closely with him, listening to his tall tales and stories of folks in the community, not only in Richmond, but nationwide. We both had seen a great deal of the same folks in our line of work, but I listened as he trashed those individuals. I never said anything to correct him or defend those whom I admired for fear of losing the job and being on the receiving end of his criticisms and observations.

One thing that always came across in the line of work that chose *me* was my compassion for others. I had friends who had died in shame, never telling anyone of their status and not allowing others to show them how much they were loved. I never wanted to hang my head in shame, although I felt like I wore a red "H" on my shirts for HIV. I genuinely cared for most of the people I served and those with whom I worked. I felt some were living in this you-owe-me mindset. The available money and funding became welfare for some. I started to disconnect.

I had clients who were living with the disease and not dying. Rather than wake up as I did and take responsibilities for their actions, some opted to sit home watching soap operas, collecting the monthly Social Security checks that barely covered the necessities of life. They knew how to work the system. When one client accessed services to pay a utility bill, in order to have spending money for the clubs, bars and latest fashions, he or she would pass that information on to their peers. Now don't get me wrong, everyone handles their status differently, but seeing as though I could get my ass up every morning to punch a clock and deal with drama, why couldn't they? On second thought, it wasn't my money so I really didn't care.

Being back in Richmond and working in the HIV/AIDS field, I had to stretch and bend when it came to telling folks what I did for a living. I wasn't ashamed by any means, but it sounded so much better and easier to explain that I worked providing services to underserved populations, than case management for those living with HIV. It was easier to slide that in conversation when I met someone, so they wouldn't assume I was positive.

On weekends, I hung out with friends, still doing shots of tequila and driving home from the bars slightly inebriated. I was the life of the party on the nights I went out. I entertained everyone with stories and discussed freely and openly the sexual rides I had taken. For some who listened, I was pegged the whore of Babylon; for others, I received their numbers slipped to me on the matchbook covers bearing the name of the bar where we met. In the mornings, when it was time to clean out my pockets for laundry, I would look at the number and try to place the face of the individual who had given me their number for their chance at me. It was a game, a game I played well.

Sometimes—actually very few times—my friends and I did things outside the bar scene, but we always wound up there before closing to see and be seen by the patrons. I had taken to wearing sarongs in the summertime because of the heat and humidity. They were, in my opinion, far more comfortable than the pants that others were accustomed to wearing.

When I met a couple of my friends at the movies one evening, I showcased the Bataki-style print sarong I had purchased in New Mexico prior to moving back east. I could see the looks of *Oh Lord* on their faces as they handed me the ticket. I turned around so that they could get the true feel for the beautiful black-and-sunburst-inspired wear. They weren't having it. We quickly entered the movie theater, stepping over others to find three seats and enjoy the movie.

I noticed the eyes of men and women alike staring at me as we exited. I liked the attention. I never cared what folks said, whether it was a mumble under their breath or a long look, it let me know that I'd accomplished what I'd set out to do—be seen.

We wound up at the same local watering hole, sharing our reviews with others of the movie. While I loved it, one friend really didn't feel it. Then we were on to the next reason we had arrived in the first place, to get our drink on.

I swayed to the techno-music videos playing on the monitors, laughing at jokes that weren't really funny and ordering rounds of Cuervo. The one lone Corona chaser I nursed throughout the evening would not kill the sting of the tequila. By this time in my life, I had become so accustomed to the shots, it took even more to help me acquire the buzz I first felt with the concoction. Every now and again, I would drift off into my own world, as table mates shared the same stories of the same folks entering we had seen over the years. It seemed every seventh customer who entered was a new face to me and a possibility of landing a new sex partner. The thought would quickly leave as my fellow shot-callers would bring me back into the conversation and the new faces would disappear in the crowd.

I hadn't really developed a liking for anyone since I'd returned from New Mexico; the hurt that I had placed on Samuel was still fresh in my thoughts as I attempted to move on. But right before the close of business, I met the next one. His name was Theo.

∞∞

My last few boyfriends and sexual partners had been white. I found very few black men or other men of color that caught my interest in New Mexico and the guys I did meet were already involved with white men or Native Americans. So it was great to meet a brother with some substance.

My buddy, who had his finger on the pulse of everything and everyone old and new in the city, advised against it. I never listened to advice from friends; it seemed too much like the right thing to do. I had planned my work and worked my plan to meet him.

Whenever I had the opportunity to meet someone in an environment where it was loud and difficult to understand the conversation, I used my line that worked for me every time: "Are you going to be a gentleman and walk me to my car?" Theo waited a moment for a visiting friend to catch up to us and we were off to the parking lot. It was working like a charm; the polite conversation, exchanging names and eventually the telephone number. He asked me to call him when I got home and I did. When I woke up the next morning and found his number next to the bed, I was able to remember him, since we had chatted for an hour before I'd gone to sleep.

We had agreed to see each other the next day to view the first film of the series I had seen the previous night. I received the directions from him and headed over to his apartment with the DVD of the first film. We popped popcorn, had a beer and watched the movie. It was the first time I had actually had a date and nothing happened outside of what we discussed. This was strange and new to me. I decided to try it again and see what would happen.

Since Theo and I had watched the first part of the series on DVD, we agreed to a second date to see the sequel. I liked being in control of the situation and only agreed to go if I were to drive. We sat in Theo's parking lot after the film and talked. I had learned more about him over the last two days we spent together, not only on the phone but in each other's company. His friend, who was visiting from his hometown, wanted to go to Washington, D.C. for the evening and hang out, but Theo was not up to the drive. He shared with me his concerns about his friend's health and I listened. Oh shit. I knew what his suspicions were, but I allowed him carte blanche to lead the conversation.

When he finished his story, I relayed my secret to him. By this time, that initial desire to bed him had gone out of the window. In the past I had used my HIV status to discourage suitors from pursuing me. I told him what I wanted him to hear, and responded, "You don't think that's going to run me off, do you?" It would have been so much easier for it to scare him away that evening than waiting for the end a year later.

Theo and I started hanging out a good deal of time. We spent evenings chatting on the telephone, until it was time for him to walk his dog before heading to bed. On weekends, I drove across town to spend an evening with him watching movies. The first few times we would sit on the lumpy and uncomfortable futon located in his spare bedroom. After we became friendlier, he would allow me to lay my head on his chest. My hair had started growing back by this time. Whenever I let a relationship go, it also was time to let my hair go. I would separate myself from the relationship as I took razor to scalp to remove all memories.

There were times lying there that I didn't complete seeing a movie. He would play in my hair, relaxing me enough to doze off in comfort. I would awaken to realize that it was late and I needed to take my medications before I headed to bed. It would have been easier to take the meds over to his place with me, but if anyone has ever been on Sustiva, they would know how much of a mind-altering fuck it can be. Besides, I wasn't ready to go there yet.

One night I became too relaxed and fell asleep. This would be the first night I missed my drugs for the comfort of his arms. I started to grow attached to him, but fought it with all of my heart. He was too nice and too sweet, I thought, to get involved with someone like me. If I could change his feelings now, it wouldn't hurt him or me in the long run. I thought I had grown up. But of course I hadn't.

I enjoyed hearing his voice throughout the course of the day, but sometimes his calls interrupted what I needed to do to get out of there. Because the television season was coming to an end, I wanted to watch the season finales, only to have him call me during the last ten or fifteen minutes of the show. I would have to wait until the cliffhangers repeated before I could actually find out what had happened.

During this dating period, I avoided all physical contact as possible. It just was not there for me. I had gone through my withdrawal of alcohol in order to adhere to my medication treatment. But his alcohol consumption showed me the mirrored image of myself when I went out, and I didn't like it. I was doing everything right, or everything that I assumed was proper in the "perfect dating" situation, but I was not happy. I wasn't fucking; I wasn't getting fucked, not because he didn't want to, but because I didn't. I checked with my doctor to see if there was something wrong with me and whether the drugs I was taking interfered with my libido. He stated this was true for some, however, it wasn't in my case. I realized after I kissed Theo for the first time in four months, that I was holding on to something I didn't want.

I played the part of the perfect boyfriend. His love continued to grow deeper for me, yet I merely went through the motions. He was an incredible man, with a heart of gold, but I would only allow him so far into my heart. I continued this lie to my heart, spending holidays and birthdays with him. Our families met and instantly liked one another. I even convinced myself that he could and should be the one for me. Shortly after asking his family for permission, I purchased a ring to ask him to spend the rest of his life with me, but that wasn't what I really wanted. I was used to turmoil and he never gave it to me. If I got angry with him or yelled at him, he would cry and I would feel bad for what I'd done. I was hoping during my outbursts that he would take everything into consideration and leave. Hell, we weren't having sex; during the year we were together I think we masturbated no more than five times. I wasn't fulfilled—emotionally, physically or otherwise. I couldn't handle being happy, so I made myself miserable. I wanted out, but I didn't know how to let him know. I had hurt so many others in the past and his heart was pure. I didn't want to hurt him.

My out came in a visit to his mother's for her birthday. We also sat around celebrating his sister's birthday. I had become very fond of his family and wanted them to remain part of my existence, but I knew I couldn't have one without the other. To celebrate, his sister asked me to do at least one or two shots of tequila for her birthday and I did. We played cards into the wee hours of the morning. I made sure that Theo was not my card partner. I was a sore loser of games and he had a tendency to renege, causing us to lose. I was talking shit and enjoying the moment after my partner and I set both him and his brother. Theo didn't like what I had to say and immediately put me in my place. "Don't be saying that shit around my family." I played the last card in my hand, excused myself from the table and never spoke another word to him that weekend.

The six-hour drive back was a long one. I was tired and drained from acting like a bitch toward him the entire weekend, but I needed to exit this without doing more damage. We had been together almost a year and he had shared many experiences with me, showing that his love was genuine. He attended my grandmother's birthday party while I was out of town with my father and his wife attending my sister's funeral. Two weeks after Grandma's birthday, he served as a pallbearer for her funeral. He offered a shoulder to cry on when my sister passed. Although I had only met her once,

I assumed her passing would bring my father and me closer together, but it didn't. Theo encouraged me to attend the funeral with my father and his wife. When we returned, it was the last time I spoke with my father.

Theo was out of town when I received the call. I noticed the number on my cell phone was that of Della's granddaughter. She had attended the funeral in North Carolina with us and we had agreed to keep in contact after years of being out of touch. This particular Thursday night, I was not in the mood for much conversation, so I decided to wait for the weekend to return her call.

Ten minutes later, I noticed the number ringing my cell phone as that of my other sister I had just met at the funeral. We had made a pact at the funeral not to allow our father to keep us from each other. I assumed that if I were straight and married with kids, my father would have encouraged, maybe even supported, the reunion, but I was his black-sheep son, living in sin. I was not worthy of his love or that of my siblings.

I felt something was wrong. It was too coincidental that I received two telephone calls from persons attached to my father. This time when I picked up the phone it was my sister.

"You have bad news for me, don't you?" I didn't say hello, or how are you doing. I knew what this call was for.

"He's in the intensive care unit at the Veterans Hospital. They don't think he is going to make it."

I got in my car and sped to the hospital. It was late at night and I figured they wouldn't allow me in. I informed the nurse at the station who I was and that I had just received the information regarding my father.

I walked through the throng of rooms until I saw him. He was lying there, with tubes entering several parts of his body. His eyes were barely open, fluttering like butterflies to steal a peek at what was going on. I watched the ventilator go up and down as he breathed the oxygen through the tube in his mouth. His chest was uncovered, showing the scars of his previous heart operations. They had removed his prosthetic leg and as I looked at this shell of a man I called Dad, my face became wet.

I reached for the free hand that did not hold intravenous tubes. He was cold. This was the first time in my life I could recall touching this man outside of a handshake and he was cold. I listened as the doctor told me my father had suffered a pulmonary embolism. I knew he wouldn't make it. There was no need to try and convince myself otherwise. When I saw his eyes open briefly, I attempted to move so that he could see that I was there with him. Despite all the hurt and distance in our relationship, I wanted to be there for him and with him. They were taking him up for X-rays to see what damage had been done, but I didn't need to know. I knew. I stroked his now silver-and-black hair, gently leaned over the bed so that I would not interrupt the flow of his oxygen tube, and said what I had always longed to hear from him: "I love you."

ℰℛ

Theo returned that Saturday morning. I planned on picking him up from the airport around 9:45 a.m., his arrival time. I was aroused from my sleep by Della's granddaughter around 5:30; they wanted me at the hospital.

I arrived in the patient waiting room. No one was there. Della had not arrived and she would be another twenty-five minutes. I sat impatiently in the waiting room for a nurse or orderly to tell me what was going on. My other step-siblings had arrived by this time and we were escorted to a back room.

You never get used to the thought of someone dying. In the past when friends had died as a result of HIV disease, I was either out of town or had heard about it after the fact. I was given a few private moments with my father to say my good-byes to him. I didn't need that much time; I had said good-bye to my father long before this moment. Della was asked by the nurse whether she wanted the ventilator removed. Her daughter stepped in and informed her that it wasn't her decision alone, that I somehow needed to be consulted. I didn't want the responsibility. I had long been excluded from this part of my father's life and the decision was solely Della's. Before she could agree to remove all life support assistance, my father took his last breath and went home.

I didn't cry. What emotions I felt were indifferent. My father had just been called home and it left no mark on me. I headed back home after receiving a call from Theo. Yes, I would be there to pick him up.

chapter eighteen

Della barely kept me informed of the arrangements for the service. I was alerted by her granddaughter of my role and when I needed to show up. I was also given the information that family members who knew me were arriving and where they were staying. I didn't know these people. The last time that I had seen a good number of them was on infrequent trips to my birth state of North Carolina, where my father would drop me off with my grandmother and make his way to the liquor houses deep in the woods.

Everyone embraced me. They had been kept abreast of my life by my father. They knew of my travels associated with my work in HIV/AIDS. They knew about the two years I had spent in New Mexico. But I couldn't think or remember anything that my father had shared with me regarding their lives.

The service came and I was allowed to ride in the family car along with my father's other illegitimate child. We were outsiders in the car, squeezed in among Della and her adult children. As we were seated, my eyes slowly followed her to the casket for her final moment with him. I questioned the sincerity of this performance after everything I had experienced with her. She no longer had someone to yell at and treat like shit. But that was my father's decision to stay. They closed the casket and she returned to take the seat beside me.

For all intents and purposes, the service was a beautiful one. It was a celebration of my father's life and the contributions he had made to the lives of others. I listened to Della's grandchildren speak fondly of my father's first dance with one of them at her debutante ball. His face lightened on dark rainy days when her kids were around to play with him. He shared Sunday afternoons with her husband watching football and talking politics. My anger built as I tightened the grip around my sister's hand. I couldn't believe what I was hearing. It was time to show and share another side of my father's love or lack of love with the mourners.

I reached the podium and surveyed the crowd. I felt Della's eyes burn into me as I shared with the audience my memories of my father. I expressed shock at the wonderful things he had done for Della's family, because I was never privy to that side of him. I chose my words carefully so that I would not piss on his memory. Anyone with good sense could read through the venom I spewed. It was no surprise to any of them that my father and I had chosen two different paths in life, but he was my father. I loved him but at times I didn't like him because of the way he had treated me. I turned my body toward his final resting place and bid him a safe journey into that good night.

Della refused to hold my hand as I took my place alongside her during the prayer. As soon as the song and dance show was over, I headed out looking for Theo. He was there to greet me and I told him I would no longer ride in the family car. Family members and well-wishers alike sought me to thank me for my words regarding my father.

Before we could make our way through the long line of well-wishers, an elderly woman wrapped her arms around me. She shared with me that she was my father's neighbor and that he loved me. I rolled my eyes. I didn't mean to be disrespectful toward her; she had nothing to do with what I was feeling. She sensed that I felt she was feeding me bullshit. She rubbed my back as she told me my father spoke of me every day to her. I found this very difficult to believe, since I barely spoke to my own father. I was lucky enough one year to actually hear his voice on the other line of the phone as he called me and wished me happy birthday on the day I was born, as opposed to a week or two later. She grabbed me again and whispered in my ear, "I know, because I'm gay also." Then and only then did I lose it. I felt a tinge of guilt. After attempting to share with the mourners my feelings about my father, I lost it. For the first time since my father died, I finally cried. I cried not because of losing him, I cried because I wanted him to say just once, "I love you." I wanted so much to rush back in and apologize, but I couldn't. He was gone and what memories I had of him, good or bad, would remain with me.

My feelings toward Theo continued to worsen. We would spend time together, but I truly wanted to be by myself. He was scheduled to be gone for a month and it would allow us time to re-evaluate where we were before going any further. The ring I had purchased to give to him became a permanent fixture in my own jewelry box. I rarely heard from him during the month he was gone and I pretty much knew it was over.

I didn't realize how over it was until he returned and informed me of his pending relocation. He would be leaving soon and he needed to take the time left in Richmond to tie up loose ends. Not a problem to me. It was weird. When he told me he was leaving, then and only then did I want him. I was used to being abandoned, so it came as no surprise. I tried to hide what I was feeling from him. I was sad to see him go; I even tried to find a reason to stay together because I enjoyed having him in my life. But his decision was made and I was not part of it.

He visited me once or twice before his departure, but I honestly think he wanted to see my mother more so than me. I hugged him good-bye and I was out there once again.

chapter nineteen

The "final" one is the most difficult to discuss. It is that painful. He was truly what I had always wanted in life. In all the years of searching for love, he gave it to me. But I was so damaged from the others and the bad decisions I'd made that I didn't recognize love when it walked in. It wasn't a sudden revelation to me who he was; I knew him from earlier years. But it was the breath of life for me that carried me to a place where I could not recover.

I met him in 1998 on a four-day bicycle ride to raise money for AIDS services in Washington, D.C. In our later discussion, he remembered me earlier when I took my bike to have it shipped for the ride.

I felt like a loner as I walked through the halls of the opening ceremony of the ride. I saw faces of fellow riders I knew, but didn't want to intrude on their thoughts and reasons for participating. We all had our reasons. My decision was based in part to memorialize the large number of friends who were no longer with me and to prove that I had the stamina to push my body to its limits. I easily raised the required registration fees from friends, family members and co-workers. I purchased a used bike that I rarely trained with and headed to North Carolina.

I saw him speaking with a gentleman that I had grown to admire in the field of HIV/AIDS. I had learned never to question anyone's status, because there were riders of all persuasions undertaking the same task. I snapped their photograph along with many others that became treasured memories of this trip.

As we embarked on the back roads of North Carolina, there was nothing to greet you but the miles and miles of highway. Early on, packs of riders that left together distanced themselves from novice riders like me. Every now and then, a more experienced rider would glide by offering words of support, interrupting the thoughts I had. At stretches along the route, I saw no other riders or drivers and I was able to connect with myself. I was not in a race to get from point A to point B. I was in a race to discover me.

The first day of the ride saw the humidity sack quite a few cyclists, including me. The most I had done in terms of training consisted of riding my bike the six or seven blocks to and from work. So you can imagine the joy I felt in accomplishing fifty miles the first day in the beating sun.

I was happy to receive an available seat on the sag bus to take me to the first night's campgrounds. I took a shower in the portable shower trucks, found a spot under the tent and had dinner. Shortly thereafter I entered my tent and rested my aching body.

The second day of the ride brought much relief from the previous day's humidity, but it also brought torrential downpours along the route. The second day I accomplished more than I had the first day. I completed all eighty-plus miles under the watching eyes of God.

The third day started out great. I carried the see-through rain jacket I had purchased because they called for more rain. This was by far the most grueling of the four days. The route facing us over the next one hundred-plus miles consisted of rolling hills and sharp drops. If rain were in the forecast, I didn't care; I knew the coolness of the air would keep me safe from the unbearable heat of the first day. But that was not to happen. Forty miles into the ride, there was not a cloud in the sky. I was bogged down by the less-than-light rain jacket and by mile fifty-five I was taken to the next pit stop.

I was rushed to the makeshift medical unit where I was placed on a cot. My body temperature had elevated and early blood work had signaled the staff that I was dehydrated. I lowered my head and cried in defeat. I knew that I could do it; I just needed the rain to keep me cool, but it would not happen the remainder of the ride. I opened my eyes to see the rush of action going on around me and there he was. His name was Oliver.

From the low-level cot I was now lying on, he towered over me. He took the seat that was vacated by the nurse, who had left to retrieve a bag of saline to attach to the IV drip she had inserted.

I tried to explain through the sobs why I was crying when he asked me the question. He asked me to stop. He offered his time and his delay in making the next pit stop to sit with me for a few minutes until the nurse returned.

He waited with me until they placed me in the jeep to take me to the final campsite. As we pulled off and he was assured that I would be okay, he hopped on his bike and headed out on his own.

I was able to catch a quick glimpse of him at the closing ceremonies the following day after the last forty-plus miles, but I was so caught up in the emotions that I didn't get a chance to say "thank you."

I remembered the words of the speaker at the opening ceremonies, stating that over the next four days we were all going to become part of a strong community. I didn't realize how strong those ties were until I replayed the memories in my head long after the ride was over.

Everyone who participated in the ride, from the riders to the crew that worked much longer and harder hours than I had, were invited to a reunion party. It was an opportunity to play catch-up and share stories about our experience. Everyone I knew was showing photographs from the four days and I had mine in hand to share with my new friends. He was one of them.

I searched around for familiar faces and discovered Oliver. We talked and I finally had an opportunity to thank him for his kindness that third day of the ride. He was even more handsome than I remembered. There was something about him that I couldn't figure out. Something that made me want him and not in a sexual way. I hadn't experienced such generosity and it was wonderful. We exchanged numbers and vowed to keep in contact. For a short time we did. In our conversations, we talked about life. I felt comfortable enough to tell him I was positive and he never judged. He treated me with dignity and respect. I was single at the time and had hoped that I could return the favor by taking him to dinner or inviting him over for a drink one night. But he wasn't single. He lived with his partner and I knew the pain from past experiences of being involved and having someone cheat. He made it clear that he honored the commitment to his partner and I bowed out gracefully.

Seven years later I found myself in the Hampton Roads area of Virginia visiting my best friend, Andre. For three weeks running, I would hop in my car and make the seventy-mile drive to visit him to hang out. Theo and I had said our good-byes and I was tired of folks asking me about him when I went out. I didn't see any new jobs in any new cities in my immediate future, so I settled for spending this time with my best friend.

Andre and I met May 3, 1985 at Richmond's hot spot, Scandal's. We developed a friendship that weathered many storms. He was pretty much there every time I cried over a broken heart and in between the heartbreak, we found ourselves exploring moments of desire for each other. He was there longer than any of them combined.

Our friendship endured months of not talking because we were pissed at the action or decision the other made. But now we were growing into something that we had not really had: a mutual respect.

I was invited to attend a barbecue with him to celebrate the Fourth of July with his friends in Hampton. It was a varied mix of individuals ranging in age, gender and sexual orientation. The pool was filled with kids playing Marco Polo and, under the shade of the enclosed picnic table, the card sharks were playing Spades. Seating was limited, so I grabbed a few dinner napkins to place under my ass as I sat there eating on the pavement with Andre. He introduced me to his new group of friends and family that he'd acquired since teaching at the local university. At times I felt out of place in his new world, but I made the best of it.

There were faces I recognized from years gone by who had relocated to the area for a much simpler way of life. I avoided the urge to drink, as I searched for the bottles of hidden water to cool me from the heat.

Randy entered fashionably late. He was an old acquaintance from one of my previous lives. He and I had met when I was seventeen through a mutual friend and shared a common interest in music. I went there once with him, but didn't pursue it any further. The years had been good to him and over the last few weeks of me visiting Andre, I attempted to build up the nerve to tell him. He wasn't alone when he entered the back gate. I took a second look to see if my eyes were deceiving me. I checked one last time to be sure. It was the man I had waited for all of my life. It was Oliver.

It was like a dream. By this time I had squeezed myself into a children's chair, seeking relief from the pavement. Randy introduced Oliver to Andre before our eyes met. I was taken back in time as he stood over me. Although he was there, I only saw the man in the biker shorts who'd sat with me when I cried seven years earlier.

"You don't remember me, do you?" I asked, hoping that he would.

He smiled that smile. "I'm sorry if I did anything to piss you off."

I reciprocated with a smile. "You were nothing but a perfect gentleman," I responded. He reached over and shook my hand.

"Hi there, how are you?" His smile told me he remembered.

It was like picking up a conversation that had been interrupted mid-sentence some seven years ago. We shared with each other the paths our lives had taken. The torch I thought had been blown out after I found out he was involved burned brighter than any light of love I had experienced in my life. During our conversation, I noticed how he became the focus of others and he made the same observation of me. We didn't allow anything or anyone to interrupt this much-needed conversation; outside of Andre and Randy checking in on us to see if we were okay.

The evening progressed and the water I drank was replaced by the shots of tequila we shared to commemorate seeing each other after all these years. Randy participated in our toasts as we eventually agreed to all take a dip in the pool that evening. We waited until the kids had worn themselves ragged and the mothers and fathers herded them up to take them home for a peaceful sleep. I wasn't prepared to go swimming, but Randy loaned me a pair of his trunks that he kept in his gym bag. In between the catching up, and the confession of my crush on Oliver, the three of us—Oliver, Randy and me—agreed that no matter what happened that evening, we would be leaving together. We exhausted ourselves playing volleyball in the pool and continued to quench our thirst with the tequila. I said good night to Andre and left with two of the most beautiful men I had ever met.

It was a holiday weekend, let alone a Sunday, and we were unable to find a place to purchase any more to drink outside of the local bar up the street from Randy's. I was driving his brand-new car and terrified at the thought of skidding off the road. We were all more than a little tipsy and Randy was not a great navigator in the state he was in, but we made it.

We entered the sports bar and I ordered a round of shots and chasers. I think the final shot took the edge off what we had planned for the evening and how it would play out. Randy took his time, but Oliver and I were more than willing to get things started.

After finishing off the Coronas, we made our way back to Randy's house. We made it no further than the cushiony sofa before I felt hands abruptly removing my clothes. I couldn't tell who was undressing me while I kissed the other. The sofa was large enough to accommodate both of them at six-feet-plus each and me at five feet eleven. Our clothes became a mound of garments and we each sought each other's mouth for kissing.

Oliver reached into his pocket to retrieve the remainder of his coke. I decided to try a little since it had been years. There wasn't enough left in the little baggie, but he was able to secure enough on the tip of his finger to place on the tip of my tongue as he forced me to suck on his finger.

We eventually made our way to Randy's bed. Our bodies became one entangled mass of flesh as we explored each other. It was difficult to focus enough attention on one person, as we all worked toward pleasing one another. I found myself resting between the two of them at crotch level, taking both into my mouth, tasting the chlorine from the dip in the pool. I noticed that Oliver had reached for a condom and the lube, while Randy prepared me. I couldn't allow the possibility of anal sex to go any further than teasing the entrance of my hole because I had not properly prepared.

I made my way to the foot of the bed to provide much-needed back and body massages for the two, before I headed out to the backyard to have a cigarette. The two of them could continue without me for now; I would return shortly to join in again.

There was a certain calmness in the air, as I stood there on the back porch smoking my cigarette. The neighbor's back light allowed me to see my shadow and the rings of smoke I was blowing. There wasn't much room to maneuver on the small square porch, but Oliver made enough room for himself to join me and place his arms around me. He checked with me to see if I was okay with what was going on and I reminded him that it was my suggestion. His arms felt good in the early morning hours, his body pressed against mine in the moonlight. It was beautiful.

We returned to Randy for a few more minutes of rolling around and enjoying each other's bodies. Before I knew it, we had drifted off to sleep, me in the middle of a fantasy come true.

I awoke the next morning with Oliver's arm securely holding me. It was strange to feel this much affection from someone. In the past when I had experienced moments like this, all parties found respite in finding their own place to sleep. I welcomed this. I pulled his arms closer to me as he drew me closer to him. I wanted this moment to last.

But all good things come to an end. It was time for me to head back to Andre's and take my medications that I had missed from the previous night. Randy made coffee and we all took turns brewing additional pots to nurse the headaches and hangovers we shared.

This time I was relegated to the backseat of Randy's car. I agreed that I would make breakfast for everyone when we arrived at Andre's and say our so-longs. As we rode Interstate 64, I placed my head out the window reliving the hours before sunrise. I had this crazy idea that I had never entertained before: what would it look like, or even feel like, to share your life and love with two others? Was it really possible for three individuals to co-exist in a loving and mutually satisfying relationship? The thought didn't go any further after Randy made it clear that he was not over his ex. Oh well, it was a moment I wouldn't forget.

I showered once I got to Andre's before I prepared breakfast. He was well aware of my antics from the night and never once mentioned a word in the presence of company. Oliver checked on me again and I attempted to hide what I was truly feeling for him. It wasn't going to work. He was living in Washington, D.C. and I was in Richmond. I had learned by now to take moments and experiences for what they were, simply moments.

I am very methodical when it comes to cooking. I first sliced the pre-rolled sausage to fit the suggested serving size on the label. In the same pan, without touching, I placed the center-cut bacon for those who don't enjoy spicy meat as much as I do, no pun intended. While both breakfast meats slowly cooked, I removed eight large eggs and cracked them in the bowl Andre rinsed out for me. I allowed him to ignite his oven because it was tricky to figure out. I placed the large butter biscuits an equal distance apart on a pan and placed them in the oven. By the time the bacon and sausage were completely cooked, I would have mixed the four-cheese mixture of shredded cheese into the already well-beaten eggs. I placed the mixture in the refrigerator until it was needed. I placed the bacon and sausage separately and cleaned the skillet for the eggs.

I slowly cooked the eggs, ensuring that they didn't burn, but enough for the four cheeses to meld with the eggs. The timer went off, alerting me that the biscuits were ready. I placed the eggs in the serving bowl and laid everything on the counter. I was not serving anyone, hell, I just cooked.

Andre's neighbor joined us for our late breakfast. He knew that I wasn't very happy with my job at the university and suggested becoming a short order cook in the Hampton area. Everyone raved about the eggs; I was glad they enjoyed them, but it was more special coming from Oliver.

I cleared my plate and headed out for an after-meal cigarette. I was hoping that Oliver would take a hint and join me, but he was busy talking to Andre's neighbor. I didn't want to feel left out, so I took a couple of deep drags and returned to the gathering.

I wanted specifically to direct my attention to Oliver, but I didn't want others to pick up on it. I moved about, packing my things for my trip back home but wanting so much to be with him.

We hugged and said our good-byes. I whispered in Oliver's ear that I wanted to kiss him one last time and I followed him back to Randy's as he prepared to depart for Washington.

Randy had distanced himself from the night of pleasure the three of us shared, but Oliver and I were sharing moments of that experience. Randy walked around preparing for another holiday barbecue and burning a CD for my drive home. I excused myself to use the bathroom and upon exiting,

Oliver grabbed me. He startled me with his question regarding my interest in Randy. I liked them both, but I couldn't tell either of them that I favored one over the other. It was obvious where I wanted to be. I wanted Oliver. I had wanted to be there with him for the last seven years.

We said good-bye to Randy and I followed Oliver to the exit that directed me home. It was great seeing him, I thought. I didn't expect to see or hear from him for another seven years but we agreed to exchange numbers as we had done in 1998.

We stopped by the gas station for gasoline and Gatorade. I told him once again how great it was seeing him and told myself not to expect anything more. We said good-bye one more time before the traffic-packed I-64 called for me.

I cranked the house CD that Randy had burned for me, listening over and over to the one song that talked about heaven. I started to learn the words after listening to it so many times. When I traveled, I never turned on the ringer of my cell phone; I just wouldn't be able to hear it over the loud speakers. I could feel someone call me when the vibration tickled my inner thigh. I didn't recognize the number or its area code. I figured this holiday it wouldn't be a bill collector calling, so I answered. It was Oliver.

He was in a hurry to make it back to Washington and sped off leaving me in the dust. I was never a speed demon so he called to find out how much progress I was making. He continued the telephone calls until I made it safely to my door.

When I arrived at work that Tuesday after the holiday, I sought out my ray of sunshine. She was my co-worker and confidante. I needed to share with someone the beautiful night I had encountered. I was beaming. I was stepping on Cloud 9 as I recalled the events that led to my fantasy and the reunion with an old friend. I didn't know where it was going and I had no expectations, but deep inside I wanted to see him again. I waited patiently before I sent the first of many e-mails that Tuesday. I didn't want to rush anything.

From Rodney
Sent: Tuesday, July 05, 12:33 p.m.

To: Oliver

Subject: Hi Oliver, Rodney here

Hi there,

I hope this e-mail finds you well and adjusting to your first day back to work. I hope that you were able to sleep well and allow the anxieties of returning to the daily routine of work subside.

I was thinking about you and just wanted to say hello.

Respectfully yours,

Rodney

We spent the rest of the day e-mailing back and forth in between catching up on work. I was so distracted, that I decided to put everything pressing on the back burner until the next day. I figured it would keep and barely addressed any other work issues that day.

Of all the relationships that I have had, this short affair had the most impact. It wasn't the time that was committed to it; it was the pure, raw love that was felt. It was the silent love that was delivered in brief pauses of conversation that kept us up until one and two in the morning. It was the morning e-mails that greeted each of us, thanking the other for the time from the previous night. We may not have spent hours on end with each other, but the absence made our hearts grow fonder.

ഇൽ

I had already plotted my escape from the university, when I received a call after the holidays informing me that I had been selected to interview with a national organization in Washington. Finally the gods were smiling on me. During one of the many e-mail exchanges, I informed Oliver of this and we agreed to see each other, sooner than later. I arranged for the interview to take place on a Monday, so I could spend a weekend with him.

Before I saw him again, I had learned so much from our conversations. He had been single for eighteen months after six and a half years with his former partner. They remained good friends after the relationship and had planned on visiting the Big Easy, New Orleans. He shared with me the events that led to the breakup and how this time he would try to remain friends with his ex. I always wanted the person I loved to be honest with me and as I found myself falling for him, I wasn't quite ready for it.

It was our first time together since seeing each other over Independence Day. I found my patience wearing thin with the evening rush-hour traffic I was caught in making my way to his place. I was so close to being with him, yet so far away.

I sensed his excitement as he checked with me to find out how far I had gotten since his last phone call ten minutes earlier. I followed the directions as they were given and made my way to his door. I was hoping that he would still be as excited to see me as I would be to see him.

My fear melted as he hugged and gently kissed me. He had a way of saying my name that made me love hearing him say it. *Rot-knee.* He introduced me to his roommate, whom I had met years ago during my five years in the District.

We sat at the bar in his kitchen, somewhat surprised at the speed this was going. We really didn't discuss it, we just sat there happy to be with one another. We tossed back drinks and smoked weed as we continued to get to know one another. His roommate's partner came over after work to get him, and Oliver and I would have the place to ourselves.

While they continued to smoke, snort and drink, I retreated to the bathroom to take care of some personal matters. I wanted to complete what Oliver had initiated the first night we were together. I needed to prepare myself for him and that was no small task. I excused myself and did what I needed to do. I wanted this night to be special.

When it was time to end the night, I had all but prepared for what was going to take place. The final touch came in sharing a long, warm shower with Oliver by candlelight. If he decided to explore my body with his mouth, I wanted him to taste freshness and not the sweat from that day's road trip.

He joined me in the shower and I watched the droplets of water drench his beautiful body. He was thin, but toned. There wasn't an ounce of fat on his body, outside of the appendage that caught the remaining water.

I wrapped my arms around him to taste him, to kiss him. He turned me around with my backside facing him. I felt him against me as he lathered my body with the Dove body wash. We spent a great deal of time just exploring each other. I was ready and so was he.

I stepped out of the shower after him and toweled off in the bathroom. He exited quickly to his bedroom to set the mood. After I finished, I walked into the bedroom that was illuminated by the numerous candles. He placed the latest Kem CD in the Bose player and reached for me.

I walked toward him, eagerly anticipating what the night had in store for us. He slid over as he made room for me to join him. I lay next to him as he leaned forward to kiss me. I looked deep into his eyes as I shivered from the breeze blowing from the oscillating fan. For the first time in my life, with this man, I spoke from my heart. I had not prepared a speech; I didn't rehearse what I would say. Gazing into his eyes, he pulled something from my heart that I had never desired saying to anyone else before. "I never want to disappoint you."

I knew from past experiences that I had disappointed former partners and in return had been disappointed myself. I had hoped by saying this, that I was not only vowing to be a better man and potential partner in this endeavor, but also hoped that my words would prevent any disappointment from Oliver. He stopped caressing my body with his fingers. I thought I'd said something wrong. I shouldn't have exposed myself like that. Damn. He continued to look deep into my heart and soul; he knew that I meant it. He felt the words reverberate in his thoughts. The honesty that I wanted from him but was leery of, I gave to him as well. He showed me he understood where my heart was; he scooped me up in his arms and he sobbed. For the first time in my life, my wish finally came true. I made love for the very first time. As I closed my eyes, I felt it could only get better.

It did for that brief moment.

I traveled to Washington on the weekends to spend with Oliver. We didn't really plan much on these weekend get-togethers; it was enough just to be with him. We prepared meals together, showered together, made love to each other, and grew out of this seed that was planted.

As I did faithfully, I packed my bags to head up to see him. I don't know why I overpacked, it was rare that we went anywhere and no matter what I wore, it didn't faze him. He embraced me for me. He didn't ask me to change. He loved me for me. That love grew stronger when we were faced with nothing but our feelings for each other.

That Friday night I had prepared dinner for Oliver and his friends. Goat cheese is an acquired taste, so I think the pot increased the hunger pains we all felt. I excused myself to take care of what cleaning and preparation I needed, before Oliver joined me in the shower. This time when we made love, I was the one who cried. I was so overcome by the thought of this man loving me. We had been extra careful in using protection since I was positive and he had remained negative all these years. But we both wanted one time to experience the naturalness of this budding love. We both agreed to remove the condom. I never shared with Oliver what I truly experienced that night. I couldn't allow myself to be more vulnerable than I had the years past. But at the time I felt him release himself in me, I saw the fireworks and felt the electricity he shared with me the next day.

I couldn't contain what I was feeling. And simultaneously we both reached that point at the same time. There was a spark of light that flashed that night. We both saw it. It was the night the lights went out in Washington, D.C.

I thought this would be an issue for us, so fresh and at the beginning of this love affair, but when there is a connection between two people, you don't need the distractions of television or radio to interfere with silent love. We, however, ventured to the movies to cool off from the heat and when we returned to his house, I was romanced in a way I never could have imagined.

I once expressed to Oliver my desire to be romanced. Simple things made me feel special, especially when I knew it came from the heart. On one trip, he had placed a card on the pillow for me with candy. He stated that it was sometimes difficult for him to be romantic. I found this hard to believe.

When we returned from the movies to endure another night without air and only the gentle summer breeze of July, he improvised. He lit the tea candles for us to see each other. We ordered dinner from the local pizza parlor and we danced by laptop until the battery was spent. He held me close as he sang Phyllis Hyman songs to me. He made me love him all over again.

Sunday arrived and I found it most difficult to leave. We were both sad as we sat there silently, fingertips barely touching to express to each other what our hearts didn't want to say. We both knew that we were going to see each other in five more days, but the five days seemed like fifty. I didn't want to prolong the sorrowful feeling, so I decided to go as much as I hated to.

That week leading up to seeing him again, I thought about my father. If he had lived long enough to meet Oliver and actually see the happiness his son was enjoying after a lifetime of hurt, would he then be able to embrace me? It was just a thought. Or so I thought.

I was troubled by these conversations I created in my mind with my father. Oliver and I sat and he allowed me to expose myself to him. In the past when I'd shared my relationship with my father with others, I was nonchalant about it, as if it didn't bother me. Outside of my therapist's office, no one saw me shed tears about the relationship I wanted—and never had—with my father, except Oliver.

I began to peel back the layers of hurt and slowly started to share with Oliver my insecurities. The conversation also stemmed from the fact I knew he was scheduled to leave in another week to go to New Orleans with his ex. I shared through the tears, the story of my father reprimanding me for accepting a compliment from someone who said I was "pretty." I shrugged off the fact that I had never been called "handsome" in my life and I so wanted to be "handsome."

He made his way around to me and picked me up in his arms. We swayed slowly to the "Quiet Storm" that night, dancing as he picked my chin up to face him. "You are a handsome man, but you are also pretty. Don't let anyone tell you otherwise. Remember this one thing, if nothing else," he kissed my tears, "sometimes being pretty ain't half-bad."

My attitude had changed in a matter of forty-eight hours. I knew that I would not see Oliver for two weeks and I missed him already. He tried to convince me that there was nothing outside of a friendship between him and his ex, but my heart wouldn't and couldn't believe it. I had reason to believe otherwise when Oliver shared with me that his ex had expressed interest in reconciling with him. After eighteen months and the thought of Oliver dedicating his love to someone new, the ex decided to throw himself back into the picture. I respected Oliver for being honest with me and sharing this information with me. But the seeds of doubt had been planted—not only with this revelation, but also with the numerous phone calls he received from the ex, when his ex knew that I was in town visiting. The cycle was coming to an end. The use of recreational drugs and alcohol that we used to enhance the laughter we shared watching comedies, provided the needed comfort in his absence. While Oliver enjoyed the late hours of carousing in the heart of New Orleans with his ex, I became a victim of my own thoughts. The calls that used to tuck me in at night from Oliver were replaced with me picking up the telephone to ensure the line was clear. During the three-day getaway I only received one call, and what started out so beautiful and promising came down like a house of cards.

I fell and I fell hard. The feelings of bad past relationships I attempted to suppress resurfaced and the writing was on the wall. I became the most erratic I had been in my life. I didn't care. During this time, Oliver saw the real me—the side that I had pretty much shown to every other one who said they loved me. It was not a side he was used to or wanted to see.

I found myself driving fucked up in the middle of the night to the District to see him. Strike one. I refused to give him the distance he requested in order to sort things out. Strike two. I called him and told him I was going to kill myself. Strike three. Ball game over.

৪০০৪

I ran away once again. I found myself drunk and dazed with a bottle of pills. This was it. This was the last time I would allow anyone to ever, ever hurt me—whether it was intentional or not. I scribbled the suicide note and chased a handful of pills with the rum I'd purchased. I called him to tell him. I wanted him to know that he was the one who had driven me to this, no one else, but that was a line in itself. It was a combination of the others as well. The love I once had from others but never felt. It was the love I longed for from my father, and the biggest culprit in the matter, it was me. The pills began to take their effect. I began to hallucinate. In my daze, I realized that it wasn't just Oliver, it was my father, it was Michael, it was Allen, it was Jason, it was Samuel, and it was the hundreds of others that had led me here. My life flashed before me as I saw myself being fucked, fucking and being fucked over. I couldn't make out what was in front of me and I saw the one person who was most instrumental in leading me down this path.

I wiped my eyes and saw me.

chapter twenty

I was groggy when I woke up. I noticed the sunlight shining through the window, interrupting this rest that seemed eternal. My mouth was dry and I looked for something to replace the moisture of my now dry and cracked lips. I was in a private room with tubes providing me with what I needed to flush my system. I turned away from the bright lights to notice my mother standing in the doorway talking to the doctor. Seated next to me was an observer. She was assigned, along with three others, to watch me consistently and continuously for the next twenty-four hours. She saw me struggle to reach for the crushed ice I brought to my parched mouth and handed it to me. I felt like shit. And if I felt like shit, I could only imagine what I looked like. I didn't quite have my sea legs and there was no way I was going to attempt to get up from the bed to look at myself in the mirror. I thought about what had led me here to this place once again. In my mind I sifted through all scenarios, clearing the way for me to see what was really there.

I saw me.

I saw me at the age of ten reaching for arms that would never hold me the way I wanted to be held, my father's. I saw me at the age of sixteen, reaching for arms that would never hold me the way I wanted to be held. I saw myself again at the ages of twenty, twenty-five, thirty and as recently as thirty-five, reaching for arms that would never hold me the way I wanted to be held. I went to each one of them in my thoughts and searched for the words to heal them, but nothing I said offered solace. All I could do was to give each of them what they needed. I gave them the hug from arms that held them the way they wanted to be held. They were my arms. I slowly eased myself up and hugged me. I needed that hug as well.

I realized at that moment the love I wanted and needed had to come from me and no one else. Right at the moment I introduced myself to the man who would love me unconditionally for the remainder of my existence; I caught a glimpse at my disheveled look in the window and managed a smile.

Oliver was right. "Sometimes being pretty ain't half-bad."

parting thoughts

I can't tell you how this journey ends, for it is a new beginning. When I finally realized that the love I wanted and needed was always in me, I started to love. I started to love me.

I now know that it is most important to share your life and love with someone who complements what is already there, versus completing what's missing. These days when I look in the mirror, I see a man. A man who has elected to be himself. A man who enjoys himself, and most importantly, one who loves himself.

Now, don't get me wrong, I'm not there one hundred percent; I'm continuing to work on me. At times it is hard and challenging, but I'm enjoying getting to know me.

I see my life for what it is now. A life that was filled with barriers and obstacles. I found my way around them. Now as I travel, I see the light that shines all around me, because it is the light that shines within me.

One day, I'll finish the story of the second part of my journey and share with you the love I find or the love that finds me, but until then, thanks for listening.

Peace, Love & Respect
Rodney Lofton

about the author

Rodney Lofton has been a voice and face for those living with HIV for the past ten years. He has served as a keynote speaker and requested facilitator by the New Jersey World AIDS Day Celebration, the U.S. Conference on AIDS, and many other events. He has presented on lesbian, gay, bisexual and transgender issues at the National Gay & Lesbian Taskforce Conference Creating Change and the Gay & Lesbian Medical Association Conference. He is a former freelance writer with *SPICE* magazine, *Music Biz* and the African-American gay publication *The Malebox*. Lofton is also a former public relations professional, having represented the likes of Kool and the Gang, Mary Wilson of the legendary Supremes, Dancehall Reggae artist Shabba Ranks and the R&B recording group RIFF. The author is currently a columnist for the online GBMNews (www.gbmnews.com) which focuses on issues related to the African American gay community including health and entertainment. He resides in Virginia. Visit the author at www.rodneylofton.com or www.myspace.com/rodlofton.